T0341282

Get Fit for Digital Business

Is your organisation in good shape for today's digital world? Has it effectively changed the way it works to keep up with the new connected consumer? Or is it still stuck on the digital business basics, losing relevance and falling behind in the race for customers?

Get Fit for Digital Business will help you to assess where you are now, where you need to go and how you can get there. Leaning on two decades of business transformation experience, Rob Laurens describes the difference between just doing digital and being digital. He provides a practical six-step process that any leader can use to accelerate change, seize the opportunities and counter the threats that digital technology brings.

This is people-first business transformation for the real world; the way to build core strength, speed and agility throughout your organisation. Free from digital jargon and corporate gobbledegook, it's a complete framework for leaders who don't have time for an MBA in digital business – but who do want to get their teams in great shape to survive and thrive in a digital world. *Get Fit for Digital Business* will help you to create an enterprise that is not just more productive and profitable, but also happier and healthier – leaving you and your team feeling and performing better in every department.

Rob Laurens is a speaker, coach and consultant specialising in digital business. He has held frontline and board roles in several mid-market companies, set up and run a digital agency in London, and led digital transformation across 104 SMEs worldwide as eCommerce Director at a FTSE 100 company.

Get Fit for Digital Business

A Six-Step Workout Plan to Get Your
Organisation in Great Shape to Thrive
in a Connected Commercial World

Rob Laurens

LONDON AND NEW YORK

First published 2019
by Routledge
2 Park Square, Milton Park, Abingdon, Oxon OX14 4RN

and by Routledge
52 Vanderbilt Avenue, New York, NY 10017

Routledge is an imprint of the Taylor & Francis Group, an informa business

British Library Cataloguing-in-Publication Data
A catalogue record for this book is available from the British Library

Library of Congress Cataloging-in-Publication Data
A catalog record has been requested for this book

ISBN: 978-1-138–61630–1 (hbk)
ISBN: 978-0-429–46214–6 (ebk)

Typeset in Celeste and Optima
by Apex CoVantage, LLC

Contents

Acknowledgements

My sincere thanks go to Dr Dave Chaffey for his helpful and insightful comments about the draft copy of this book. My love and thanks also go to my wife Linda, whose patience with the writing process was extraordinary. Thanks also to my lovely boys, Harry and Max, who, despite being baffled as to why anyone would want to write *a book*, helped to keep me going with their wit and youthful wisdom. I am also very grateful to my friend Jim McNally for his wise words and support as well as my work colleagues past and present. Finally, last but by no means least, my thanks go to the good people at Routledge – to Amy for giving me the opportunity to be published by such a fine publisher and to Alex for her help and encouragement throughout the writing and production process.

Foreword

It's not easy being a business leader, even at the best of times. I know. I have been a director for other people's businesses and my own for more than twenty-five years. I have learnt that it's often rewarding but rarely what I would call straightforward. There are always deadlines to be met and decisions to be made. Leaders all over the world face a myriad of challenges on a daily basis in their quest to acquire and retain profitable customers. Economic slowdowns, high business costs, changing regulations, employee skills gaps, intensive competition at home and abroad . . . I could go on.

Finding time to put up the periscope and scan the business horizon can be difficult in the melee of day-to-day business as usual, particularly in small to medium-sized organisations (SMEs) where "all hands on deck" is the rule rather than the exception. There's always plenty to think about. In addition to managing the activities within our control, we also need to deal with the proverbial "events", the things that happen in the world that ripple into the orbit of our organisations.

So far, in my working life, both in the UK and abroad, my colleagues and I have faced business disruption from a variety of external forces: epidemics, financial crises, political upheavals, natural and transport disasters, strikes, civic unrest, terrorism, coups, and all-out wars. Such events come and go, testing our resilience – and fortunately not every industry is so exposed to the winds of global catastrophes as some of those I have worked in.

But there has been one disrupter that has caused more seismic change in business than any, or all, of those events. It is something that affects every organisation and it won't go away. Instead it continues to reshape the way the world works – and with it, the world of work. It has changed, and continues to change, not just business, but global societies. Its effects and implications are all around us, from politics to education, entertainment and culture.

That disrupter is, of course, digital. It has made leadership even more challenging by adding new and ever-changing layers of complexity into the way we do business. I speak from personal experience because, after the early part of my career in what we might call the analogue business world, I have spent the past fifteen years helping leaders to adapt their organisations to the challenges and opportunities that digital has brought into the marketplace.

In that time, I have worked with and within scores of SMEs and mid-sized companies, as well as famous museums and an industry-leading plc. I've been the client, hiring agencies and consultancies, and I've been on the other side of the fence, running them. I've worked in Europe, Africa, Australia and the United States. I've seen the same thing everywhere – smart business leaders struggling to get to grips with digital. So, as a coach and consultant, I help them to get a clear-eyed view of their future, frame the digital challenge and plan the steps to build their capability to thrive in the new business world. You could say it has become my vocation.

I am particularly passionate about working with SMEs, those businesses with ten or more employees, but less than 250. So, I have primarily written this book for their leaders – or anyone with ambitions to join their ranks. I prefer "SME" to the alternative of "SMB", as used in the United States and other countries, because not of all of those enterprises are businesses. Many are charities, not-for-profit organisations, non-governmental organisations, and other institutions. Digital doesn't discriminate, and so, for the purposes of this book, nor do I.

To my mind, there is something heroic about the men and women who lead these organisations, collectively the world's largest employers and the engines of economic growth. Leading any enterprise is not the easy option. The hours aren't great. Holidays can be infrequent. On a bad day, juggling multiple tasks, it can feel like running a marathon on a treadmill; a long, exhausting slog on which, despite your best efforts, you don't seem to be getting very far.

Add a game changer like digital to the mix and leaders can feel they are running a marathon uphill on a surface of shifting sand. It becomes harder still when, as an organisation, you have gradually drifted out of shape, no longer in tune with the habits and demands of the modern connected customer.

SMEs play an increasingly vital role in society as a whole, particularly as the strength of digital superpower brands continues to grow. Although a few SMEs may eventually become big enough to mount a challenge to them individually, increasingly I am beginning to see them as a kind of tacit rebel alliance, an informal resistance to the growing domination of commerce by the "Death Star" digital giants.

That may sound a little overdramatic. But, in addition to the almost weekly news reports of large retail chains shutting up shop, many small businesses have gone to the wall with far less fanfare, often as a result of the digital superpowers turning their all-seeing eyes onto a new market segment that they see as ripe for disruption. Each time the shutters go down on an SME, livelihoods are lost and tax revenues depleted.

It's not just the traditional booksellers, travel agents and video rental shops. That's old news now. They were not special cases, they were simply the first. Now it's everything, everywhere. Whatever you do, whatever your product or service, the hot breath of the digital big bad wolves is likely to be felt at some point soon, if it hasn't already.

The digital model is now well proven. It has shown that the future contains fewer middlemen, more direct to consumer selling, more anytime, anywhere services, and faster product and service delivery. It has allowed consumers to instantly access information, to weigh the value of products and services by consulting an online expert or seeking out the wisdom of the crowd. We can now compare prices and easily connect with suppliers wherever they may be. And all from the palm of our hands.

Most of us have embraced this new world as consumers. It has made our lives easier in many ways. But that doesn't stop us being sentimental. I was in the pub recently listening to a friend lamenting the loss of yet another household name on the high street and in shopping malls – apparently the latest casualty of the so-called Amazon effect. He waxed lyrically about the love he felt for the brand and how he felt its loss like that of an old friend. Perhaps raising an eyebrow, I asked him when he had last shopped there. "Oh . . . yes . . . well . . . hmm . . . probably about two years ago", he replied somewhat sheepishly.

The truth is he, like me, has an Amazon Prime account. I know he compares prices on Google Shopping, but his default supplier for most things is now Amazon, because it makes his life a little bit easier. For him, retail therapy means getting his shopping done as quickly and painlessly as possible.

But he also wants to buy the best that he can afford, so he also researches online, reading the reviews by industry influencers and buyers alike. He takes the same attitude whatever he's shopping for, from cars to software to professional services. Amazon has changed his expectations of good service. He won't deal with any supplier who fails to match their standards.

Recently, he moved house using an online service to sell his property. He has just bought the Amazon Echo device, despite being a little wary of having a "spy in the camp", as he puts it. He simply couldn't resist the lure of having the latest gadget and is happy to use his voice to get information or buy products. (He is a terrible typist.) He streams box sets and films on Netflix, uses Facebook, LinkedIn, subscribes to various Twitter feeds, posts photographs on Instagram and is a member of several WhatsApp groups. He also wears a fitness band and has become somewhat obsessed by the metrics of steps and the amount of deep sleep he gets each night.

His kids, like mine, buy and sell fancy hoodies and trainers on a peer-to-peer social shopping app, a kind of cross between eBay, Pinterest and Instagram. They stream their entertainment and rarely watch traditional TV. They regularly play online games, often taking on opponents sitting in bedrooms across the world.

On that basis I'd say that, ostensibly at least, he "gets" digital. As well as being a good friend, he is also my legal adviser, and is a senior partner in a firm of solicitors. A couple of days after our conversation in the pub, he asked me to send him a letter confirming some details of a business arrangement with a third party. When I incredulously said "a letter?" he then actually suggested a fax.

I recount this anecdote because it illustrates an interesting digital dichotomy. As consumers we have all embraced digital tools and techniques with almost indecent enthusiasm. And yet, in a work environment, we struggle to make that change with quite the same speed and verve. In my friend's case, he seemed unable to make the connection between the way he approached all things digital as a consumer, versus his habits and attitudes as a business leader. It is as though he a digital blind spot, using the long-held traditions and habits of his profession as a kind of unconscious shield against change.

I think another reason for the difference in his digital behaviour is that it's much easier to embrace change as an individual. There are no committees to convince or costs to incur. We simply try something, a new app or social media platform for instance, and, if it's easy and we like it, we adopt it. Using it then becomes habitual – our default behaviour.

In business it's just easier to keep doing the things we've always done in the way we've always done them. Business is a team game. Change becomes exponentially harder when other people are involved in a professional setting. It's not just colleagues, but also partners in our value chains – suppliers, agencies and increasingly customers themselves.

When you suggest change you're messing with people's professional function, their existing priorities, power bases and perhaps even their livelihoods. People are very wary when they perceive that something new could affect their bread and low-fat spread. Just using someone else's mug can cause an major incident in some offices. After a while, when thoughts of change have been kicked into the long grass of our organisational consciousness, we can stop noticing. We shrug our shoulders and accept the status quo because "that's what it's like in our company/industry".

There's an unpleasant urban myth which says that if a frog is placed in a saucepan of boiling water, it will jump out, but if it is placed in cold water that is slowly heated, it will not perceive the danger. Instead, it will stay in the saucepan until it is boiled alive. According to biologists, this is an apocryphal tale. However, the moral is clear and highly relevant to digital; namely, that any enterprise of any size or area of activity, can fall foul of "boiling frog syndrome", unable to detect the slippery slope of gradual change until it is too late.

Many industries have had a good run. For some, things have been pretty much the same for decades. The way they do business, what they sell and how they sell it has become deeply ingrained. Job titles, organisational structures, distribution networks, and sales and marketing techniques have remained almost unchanged throughout many industries.

Usually a bit of digital activity gets bolted on – a shiny new website, random stuff posted on social media, dull emails sent to customers – and everyone can rest assured that they are "doing digital". But digital remains a business sideshow for them, rather than the main event. In other words, they trundle on *doing* digital rather than *being* digital.

In some sectors you can get away with that for a time, maybe even a long time. But in the background, the connection with customers and relevance in the market is being inexorably eroded. To succeed in the future will take more than the digital basics. It won't be enough to simply shift more advertising online, build a mobile-friendly website and digitise a few manual processes. At this point in the twenty-first century, it's become a bit more fundamental than that.

Let's change the metaphor. Rather than boiling frogs I prefer the analogy of getting physically fit (and I expect you do too). Physically we can drift out of shape so gradually that we, and the people who see us regularly, hardly notice that it's happened. Or it might be that we have noticed, but are in denial about the condition we are in and the likely consequences of that somewhere down the track. Perhaps we want to take some action, but simply don't know where to start. Maybe we are concerned about the risk of injury or even a heart attack. Whatever the reasons it's important to get off the back foot and begin to be proactive.

Using the analogy of getting fit for digital change helps us to get away from the disturbingly dull dialogue of digital change and "transformation". It helps us to think differently about the challenges and opportunities and provides an antidote to the buzzwords and jargon that tend to surround the topic. In my experience hands-on business leaders do not have the time or inclination to work through a virtual MBA in digital transformation. But they do want to avoid a long and expensive process of trial and error.

I know that most people have had their fill of bamboozling corporate gobbledegook, acronyms and the confusion of multiple names for what are essentially the same things. In my experience, leaders and their colleagues want practical, actionable and realistic advice that is described in plain language, without being dumbed down. So that is what I have tried to deliver in this book. Where I have used industry terms, I've provided short definitions, so that when somebody throws one of these buzzwords into the conversation you'll know what on earth they're talking about.

I also like the fitness analogy because it helps to create a more positive narrative about change. Digital is of course often characterised as a looming threat in the form of disruptive competitors with new business models. As such, many leaders and employees approach it with trepidation and even fear.

But I don't think that leaders should simply view digital as something that they need to defend against. With the right approach it is much more about opportunity. It is a way to consistently find more leads, convert more prospects into customers, build your reputation, get closer to your buyers and create a happier, less stressed workplace. But unlocking that opportunity takes thought and planning. It won't happen unless leaders actively work at it to make it happen.

Some of the tools I describe and recommend are long-established business best practice – tried and tested techniques that are well worth revisiting in the context of digital disruption. For example, I recommend that leaders should look again at their business vision to ensure that it is still relevant in a digital business age. Other techniques described in the book, such as customer journey mapping, are newer, emerging as best practice to respond to the new digital paradigm.

The purpose of this book is to bring all these elements together into a simple, step-by-step self-help programme for leaders; one that covers both the process and key components of what I call "getting fit for digital business". It's a framework that will ensure that leaders can effectively marshal and co-ordinate the many moving parts of digital into a cohesive approach that is right for the unique requirements of their individual business.

It is also a call for action. Getting ready for an increasingly digitised world is not something that can sit on the back burner any longer. It's time for all leaders to act decisively because it can be a slow process to get fit and in great shape for the modern business world. No organisation can change everything at once. A "Big Bang" approach will usually cause a lot of collateral damage. It takes a sustained focus and effort. Just like perfecting a golf swing, a tennis shot or a dance move, it takes patience and persistence to build new muscle memory within organisations.

Most of all, I want show how taking a planned approach to digital is achievable for all enterprises, whatever their size or scope. Of course, unlike big businesses, most SMEs lack the resources to create digital innovation centres or hire expensive management consultants to drive change. But that doesn't mean getting fit for digital is out of reach.

I know from experience that, by taking a step-by-step approach and focusing on one workout at a time across the six components of digital fitness, the barriers to change can be overcome and the common pitfalls can be avoided. It's worth it. Helping your enterprise to evolve is a better way to grow and increases the odds that your firm, not some new digital disruptor, will prevail in your sector or niche market.

Leaders don't need to be experts in all areas of digital to drive change. They simply need to be good leaders, adapting themselves and their organisations to meet the demands of an always on digital marketplace. Any leader willing to ask the right questions and take a planned approach can make it happen. They can inspire their team to buy in, contribute and collaborate to modernise their business and secure its future.

In truth, getting fit for digital business is more about humans than technology, whether an enterprise is a team of ten or 249; it should be focused on the people who lead organisations, the people in their teams and the people who actually buy their products and services. Of course, technology is a pretty essential element. But it simply plays a supporting role as an enabler.

Like getting physically fit, getting an organisation into great shape for digital takes some commitment and application. But above all it should be an enjoyable business reboot; an energising exercise of developing core strengths, speed and agility, one that will help your enterprise to feel and perform better in every department.

Today that is the path to faster growth, increased productivity and bigger profits. Not only that, but it is the only way to create a healthier, wealthier business that is better to lead, buy from, work with and work within.

The book is divided into four short parts:

Part 1 reflects on where we are now in the digital business revolution, how we got here and where we are going next, sharing my own experience of the realities of digital transformation.

Part 2 covers the get fit for digital business six-step process. You'll learn practical techniques including how to warm up your team for change, overcome resistance and create a future vison that people really buy into.

In Part 3 you'll discover the six components of digital fitness and the workouts every enterprise should do to modernise their business approach.

Part 4 rounds off the whole get fit programme with a summary of how you can to culturally embed the changes you make, developing the business stamina and muscle memory needed to make your organisation increasingly productive and relevant to today's connected customers.

Throughout the book you'll also find some digital workout tips to help you to focus on the most important aspects of each fitness component.

Bibliography

Dennis, Steve (2017) Assessing the Damage of "the Amazon Effect". *Forbes* (19 June). Available at www.forbes.com/sites/stevendennis/2017/06/19/should-we-care-whether-amazon-is-systematically-destroying-retail/#1e57478d6b1f (accessed 13 March 2018).

Inam, Henna (2013) Leadership and the Boiling Frog Experiment. *Forbes* (28 August). Available at www.forbes.com/sites/hennainam/2013/08/28/leadership-and-the-boiling-frog-experiment/#5f56d7506e21 (accessed 11 January 2018).

Part 1

Introduction

The only constant is change

Before we dive into the programme, it's worth pausing to reflect on where enterprises were, and how far they've already come in changing the way they do business. When I started working, some time ago now, the primary way to be found by customers was by way of the Yellow Pages. That chunky printed book was effectively the search engine for the pre-digital world, used by people who knew what they wanted and were actively looking for it.

Database marketing enabled some precision in our marketing, helping us to retain and upsell customers. Some of us used direct mail to target prospects, test our customer propositions and track responses through codes and dedicated telephone numbers.

But at that time, most of our marketing was anything but precise. We placed adverts in publications and places that matched our target market's broad demographic profile. We tracked marketing performance with the question "where did you hear about us?" Market testing was also an expensive and blunt instrument, with occasional focus groups acting as our objective eyes and ears on the ground.

Looking back, in customer terms, we were comparatively blind and profoundly deaf. As a consequence, given that we were relatively isolated from our customers, we thought less about them and more about our products and services. In those days, bike couriers were a common sight in reception, as we physically sent information to one another. I can still hear the exasperated cries of "where's that bike?" We thought we were moving pretty fast, you see.

Now we work to ensure that our websites are visible when consumers type relevant keywords into search engines. We transfer documents, artwork and some products electronically. We can track almost every-thing, everywhere. And, because "bits" travel faster than bikes, the pace has ramped up considerably.

Over the past couple of decades digital technology has certainly changed the way we work. As a change leader, getting wider leadership buy-in for many of these changes wasn't too difficult, and was typically based on no-brainer, cost-saving business cases. Implementation was also relatively easy, as we were simply digitising existing business processes. What excited business leaders most in the early days was the internet's potential to dra-matically reduce costs (print and people), shifting customers to online self-service as a fast way to boost profits.

But the introduction of online selling wasn't without drama. Perceived as an internal competitor, it could be a hard sell to vested interests within an organisation. People's enthusiasm for change varied, but there was plenty of pushback, particularly from existing sales departments.

In the early days of digital, I remember call centre colleagues refusing to ask customers for their email addresses, because it threatened to cut them out of the sales loop and impact the commission they could earn. There were also regular cases of customers being advised that it was "safer" to book by phone. It became clear that there was a rearguard battle being fought by our sales people, who, understandably, felt threatened by the growth of ecommerce. Their mood was not improved when discounts were offered to customers who bought online, rather than in stores or over the phone. As leaders, we had failed to get buy-in and we risked making ene-mies of our own people.

Sales and marketing staff were the first to be impacted by the internet, but not the last. Soon product departments began to feel the heat. I worked as an ecommerce director for a mid-market travel company in 1999 and led the development of one of the UK's first flight ticket booking engines. Our target market was students and our product complex. The variety of air fares and accompanying terms and conditions was bewildering. This wasn't a huge issue when experienced sales staff were selecting products for cus-tomers face to face or on the phone, but it threatened to derail our online selling goals before we had even begun.

When we launched the booking engine it was far from perfect for customer use. Lack of time, money and that product complexity saw to that. We were, I suppose, "working lean" and "launching beta" with "mini-mum viable products", although we'd never heard of those things. It just seemed the most practical way to get things done in a digital business environment.

Inevitably there were some naysayers. "Nobody will use it", they said. "Customers might book cheap tickets but they won't book expensive long-haul tickets. They won't be prepared to enter their payment details online". But we enjoyed strong support from our managing director, so we got the booking engine built and launched.

Customers had to work hard to get through the clunky booking process. But amazingly they did. I still remember the excitement of coming into the office in the morning and seeing that scores of bookings had been made and paid for by customers overnight. A trickle turned into a flood. This gave us the confidence to push the business to deliver a simplified product to boost sales further. In practice this required that we renegotiate our airline contracts, something that a busy product department could have done without. But it rose to the challenge and online sales continued to grow at an extraordinary rate.

We also quickly realised that we needed a constant supply of fresh and interesting content, so we started asking our staff to provide accounts of their trips, as well as partnering with guide books and freelance writers. Students were recruited (quite easily) to travel around the world equipped with digital cameras, new technology at that time, so that we could get daily updates on their experiences to share with our content-hungry audience.

We began to segment our database of students so that we could update them by email with regular content that was particularly relevant to them; for example, we knew that medical students often went on electives to long-haul destinations, so we published guides that would help them to get organised for their trips.

Over the course of the next ten years, as a leader in both business and agencies, I led the design of multiple websites, which delivered increasing levels of functionality, richer content and more user-friendly designs. My teams and I planned and implemented more sophisticated customer relationship strategies and worked to understand the mysteries of search engine optimisation (SEO) and the developing pay per click advertising platforms on those search engines. These innovations quickly yielded a competitive advantage. We had, for a while at least, got ahead of the game and it was working well for us all.

At one company, I led the transition from direct mail to digital marketing strategies. In less than a year, millions of pieces of direct mail had been largely replaced by online channels as our primary method of customer acquisition. It was good news for everybody except the printers, giving us better results at reduced cost. It was also more environmentally sustainable, something that had entered public consciousness and created a backlash against so-called junk mail. Better targeting also had the effect of helping us to acquire customers who stayed loyal for longer, because they were a better match for our product.

Along came a spider

[Bot: a computer program that works automatically, especially one that searches for and finds information on the internet.]

We had entered the new age of the algorithm. Search engines and their spider bots crawling the web proved to be a game changer. It soon became obvious that some businesses were feeling the impact of the web in general and the consumer use of search engines in particular. When I was running a digital agency in London in the early 2000s, we had a client who had recently purchased a medium-sized travel insurance business. They had paid a market price for it that reflected its well-established brand and leading sales performance.

But a problem emerged. A new market entrant, with a new business model, had disrupted the market and was beginning to eat my client's lunch. That competitor was one of the early digital specialists, expert in attracting prospects from search engines and converting them into customers with great websites. They were first and foremost digital marketing experts, rather than traditional insurance brokers, and used their search engine optimisation (SEO) skills to put their product in front of qualified buyers. This allowed them to reach people actively searching for travel insurance at a much lower cost compared to traditional marketing techniques.

It was clear that my client needed to adapt quickly in order to grow web sales and acquire more new customers at a lower cost. We got to work and researched the keyword combinations people were using to find insurance products. Then we optimised the website to rank highly in Google and the other search engines (back then Google had yet to become the digital superpower it is today and other search engines still had a good share of users).

Even then, making a website visible on the first page of search engines results for lucrative insurance keywords was a competitive and difficult business. But we had some of the best SEO people in the business and soon the website was riding high in the organic search engine results – the ones you don't pay for and users click on most.

Getting seen by prospects wasn't our only challenge. Price was also an issue. The cost of our client's policies was not comparable to the new competitor, who had kept their customer acquisition costs low by investing in SEO rather than expensive print and TV advertisements. Our solution was to offer the lowest price and encourage our website visitors to click on the links we provided to our competitors' websites. "Go compare and check our claim" became our customer call to action.

We earned money on each click users made through a partnership deal with the company serving up these link ads to our visitors. It was enough to subsidise our costs and make a good margin on policies sold at a lower price online. We were, if you like, an early form of price comparison site. If we'd been a bit brighter then, we might have realised that price comparison would become a business model in its own right. Ho hum. In any case, those tactics wouldn't work today. Things keep changing in the digital world, demanding constant innovation to keep up, get ahead and stay ahead.

Social services

When social media came along it was harder to make the business case, unless you were an established brand with big budgets taking every opportunity to stay in the minds of your customers. In the early days of social media, I was working as an ecommerce director for the world's largest travel company, leading digital transformation for a portfolio of over 100 SMEs across the globe.

Initially I had to convince leaders that social media wasn't simply about people watching cats play the piano. It soon became clear that social media had the power to turn our customers into our best and most cost-effective marketing channel, as people shared their travel experiences with their friends and family.

No traditional marketing techniques can compete with the authentic voice of the customer as expressed in their videos, photos or written content. Simply nudging customers into sharing their content proved to be very effective in both marketing reach and cost terms. Although the production values may sometimes have been lacking, the emotional impact of user-generated content on their friends and family began to translate into increased business. All we had to do was encourage and facilitate that natural human behaviour of sharing experiences.

[Social listening: the process of monitoring digital conversations to understand what customers are saying about a brand and industry online.]

Working in the travel industry, it was relatively easy to make the case for social media, as it was quickly taken up by our customers. By using the emerging "social listening" technology we could show our colleagues that social media had become a turbo-charged "recommend a friend", always the most efficient and cost-effective force in marketing.

We later created our own social platforms, linking with Facebook, that gave our prospects the opportunity to view videos, photos and blogs from previous customers (all of whom gave their permission, of course). They were also able to "meet" their travel companions online before they departed on one of our tours. In other words, we worked with our customers to create more value for all of us.

Next came the introduction of customer reviews, which quickly proved to be a powerful conversion booster, once the business had been persuaded that the benefits outweighed the perceived risks of any negative feedback. And there were more innovations to come.

Mobilising for a new world

The rapid take-up of smartphones and tablets launched the next wave of change. Getting buy-in to make our websites work well on all screen sizes wasn't too difficult. Mobile sales charts were shaped like a hockey stick and we now had good analytics running on our websites. Tracking allowed us to easily prove that an increasing number of our prospects and customers were viewing and buying our products on mobile devices.

Implementation, however, proved more challenging compared to getting buy-in. Making our complex websites mobile-friendly, or "responsive" as we say in the trade, wasn't easy. It required additional investment and we were pushing the limits of our traditional budget allocation. Something had to give. We simply had to stop doing some of the things we'd always done in order to free up budget and human resources so that we could develop our digital capabilities.

The obvious choice was to cut back on the high cost of brochure production and distribution. But we knew it would be tough to get buy-in from some of our stakeholders. Brochures were sacred cows in the travel industry, just as catalogues were or are in many other sectors. They may still have a place in the marketing mix for some, but, for me, the printed brochure began to symbolise the fundamental difference between old and new ways of working.

For many companies, the annual production of the brochure or catalogue was the one event that brought people together from across the organisation. It was really the only time that product, pricing, and sales and marketing people pitched in together, collectively contributing to a frantic month or two of production. After the thing went to print everybody retreated happily to their functional enclaves. It was a set and forget mindset, reflecting the finality of the printed page. Once it was done it was done, finished for another year – cue sighs of relief all round.

[Always-on marketing: a term to describe the change in emphasis from periodic marketing campaigns to a continuous process of marketing across channels to attract qualified prospects to your website.]

But, of course, that can't happen anymore. Digital requires that we are now "always on". That means different functional teams need to work together every day, all year long, constantly collaborating to innovate and optimise the product, proposition, price and customer experience.

Brochure production also highlighted the struggle of teams working simultaneously on old school tasks, while trying to get to grips with all the new opportunities that the web had made possible and increasingly compulsory for business success. Not only did this increase their workload, but they were also on a huge learning curve, working out on the job how best to develop content, how to make websites easier for customers to use and how to communicate engagingly with customers by email.

Our solution back then was to secure commitment, from a willing subset of our SME managing directors, for the transfer of an increasing proportion of budget from brochure printing and distribution to digital marketing activities. This was something of a "lighthouse project", a way of demonstrating the benefits of change in order to accelerate the pace of digital transformation.

To sugar the pill, we developed brochure app technology centrally to help each business to create digital brochures at a very low cost. This app, primarily designed for tablet users, made use of the businesses' existing printed brochure artwork, but enhanced the content with videos and additional photography. The back-lit images were more attractive and immersive when viewed on an electronic device. This helped to reduce resistance from those within each business who felt that cutting back on brochure production would negatively impact sales.

It wasn't just a leap of faith. We had that analytics data showing us that more and more of our website users were using tablets and smartphones. Nevertheless, we were all relieved to see that customers quickly embraced the ebrochure, enjoying its enhanced features and instant access, as opposed to waiting for it to drop through their letterbox in a printed form. It also led to an increase in conversion as the ebrochure provided direct links to further content and easy booking options on the website.

It was the eponymous win-win, improving customer experience and driving more sales while reducing production and distribution costs. It helped to get us off the blocks and we were able to reduce traditional brochure budgets dramatically over a two-year period. That ringfenced money was then reinvested in the creation of industry-leading websites with the best content, functionality and usability. That was the ultimate objective. For my team, the brochure app was merely a stop-gap, a way of getting buy-in, mitigating inertia to change, and getting budget allocation more focused on developing and continually optimising our core digital platforms and channels.

Confronting the challenge of change

As the evolution of digital technology relentlessly accelerates, humans, at least collectively in workplaces, have struggled to keep pace with three key drivers of transformation: changing consumer demand; changing technology; and changing competition. It's not simply that the organic evolution of internal human processing power takes a little longer than the creation of ever more powerful silicon chips – although a Moore's Law for humans would be based on a somewhat longer timescale (which is why we started building digital machines in the first place). It has much more to do with how we prepare and organise ourselves within businesses to respond, and keep responding, to the frenetic cadence of modern business life.

Most organisations have adopted new technologies of course. But they have also frequently left their people struggling to cope with the strictures of old mindsets, traditional structures and old back-end IT systems. You can create any number of websites and apps, but if you fail to fix what's behind them, it's going to be nigh on impossible to create an integrated joined-up business delivering a joined-up customer experience. That's important, because online customer experience has become just as big a part of people's buying decisions as their trust in the brand and the quality and price of the actual products and services which they are buying.

A failure to tackle the fundamental issues that digital gives rise to can take its toll on an enterprise, disappointing customers and putting a big strain on its human resources. This makes it difficult to keep up, consequently creating unnecessary tensions and stress. Technology is a good example; when an enterprise's systems have a modern web front-end which is barely on speaking terms with the legacy back-end systems, making improvements to the online customer experience is difficult. Whenever I see this in an enterprise, it reminds me of a pantomime horse, whose front and back legs are so out of kilter that the company can only stagger down the road, bumping into hurdles, watching enviously as more agile competitors take them at a gallop.

Team morale and individual motivation inevitably suffer. The ability to attract new talent declines. Digital business stars gravitate to the organisations where the conditions for success already exist. Most do not want to spend their time fighting internal battles or wrestling with technical systems that resemble a congealed bowl of spaghetti.

That leaves leaders stuck between a rock and a hard place, having to choose between hiring digital immigrants with a limited knowledge of the web or digital natives with less commercial experience or know-how. An intimate understanding of the latest social app as a user does not make anyone a digital business expert. Perhaps understandably, when confronted by this dilemma, many companies simply decided to outsource almost everything digital to an agency.

Inevitably there was, and still is, tension between new and old ways of thinking. Business leaders began to feel that the geeks were taking over and that they were getting pushed out of the loop, somehow disenfranchised in their own domains (pun intended).

Looking back, I also remember the pivot point when the critical mass of business people moved to embrace digital from a position of initial scepticism. It was reminiscent of Elisabeth Kübler-Ross's famous five stages of grief, whereby after the loss of a loved one, people move from denial to anger before acceptance. That moment of truth prompted something of an existential crisis in the collective mind of many organisations, as leaders debated whether they needed to become less traditional and perhaps more like a technology company and/or content publisher.

When I took on my first role in ecommerce in 1999, I was initially regarded as a bit unhinged by senior colleagues for embracing the web with quite so much enthusiasm. Looking back, I was taking a bit of a risk, as I had been leading a large division as general manager for this company at the time. But I had become utterly convinced that the internet was a business game changer.

In this new role, I was sitting in a new office somewhere between IT and marketing; both physically and metaphorically. At first no one paid too much heed to this newfangled ecommerce and they were happy to let me and my growing team get on with it.

But understandably, it didn't take long for the functional heads in these disciplines to wonder whether perhaps the internet *was* the coming thing. They began to realise that they should be more involved at least, and perhaps try to take some ownership to protect their spheres of influence.

I participated in this battle for ecommerce functional supremacy several times over the next ten years or so, as IT made the case that they should lead because "it was all about technology", while marketing argued that it was primarily "about communications". Nobody thought to specifically mention the customer.

Of course, it turned out that successful ecommerce required input from both marketing and IT . . . and the sales team, the product team, the human resources department (HR) and finance . . . in fact everybody in the business. We realised we needed to get better at publishing high-quality content, and to gain an understanding of how we could use technology better to increase efficiency and improve the buying experience of our customers. And we knew we had to do it without losing sight of who and what we were – providers of exceptional travel experiences to real people, our customers.

Most of all we needed to find ways of turning that realisation into action. That required the emergence of champions and evangelists, both for the emerging technology and for the customer. We needed change agents, ready, willing and able to work with, and challenge, colleagues across functions, before building consensus to get the digital tasks done. Those people had to be prepared to put their heads over the parapet and take the risk of being the nuisance who was disrupting the comfortable status quo. It was not always a comfortable place to be and the best leaders recognised that.

So, what did I learn from those early days of my digital business journey? Well, I learned that technology, relatively speaking, is the easy bit. The real hard work was making the case and getting buy-in for organisational change and innovation. I learned that we needed to innovate incrementally, piloting new digital initiatives and using data – in the form of customer feedback, website analytics and most of all sales figures – to prove that such changes made positive impacts on the bottom line.

I began to understand how to make change happen, by focusing on practical ways to shift thinking and spending from traditional activities to new and better ways of serving our customers. I started to realise that the old hierarchal ways of managing business as usual didn't work in a digital business world, in which teams needed to be freer to test, learn and execute in a faster and more agile way.

I think I also learnt to balance empathy with assertiveness, and to appreciate that many people are understandably nervous about change and any proposed move away from the traditional tried and tested ways of doing business. It also became clear that, particularly in those crunch moments, sponsorship and support from the very top is not just helpful, but absolutely essential.

Most of all I learned that making change happen is not an overnight "transformation". It requires a change in mindset from leaders and their teams. It requires a willingness to work more closely together, because it affects everybody in an organisation, whatever their function. It demands a renewed focus on customers, and a joined-up, fully co-ordinated approach across multiple areas and many moving parts.

In summary, what I really learned is that getting fit for digital business is principally about people. It's about using technology to enhance those people – leaders, their teams, value chain partners and customers – giving them the everyday superpowers they need to create more value together.

To successfully make all that happen requires a framework and a positive narrative to get everyone bought in and fully committed. Making serious change happen while keeping the show on the road is challenging. It has been compared to changing a wheel while the car is still moving. That's tricky of course, but it is doable with the right skills and good teamwork. It's also very necessary.

So, how do you go about it? Where do you start and on what do you focus your efforts? Which new skills, tools, processes, business habits and techniques do you need to get there? How do you effect positive change when resources are limited and the pressures of "business as usual" remain? We will get to that shortly. But first, let's get a shared understanding of what digital actually is.

What is digital anyway?

We've only just got going and I've already used the term "digital" a lot. I don't think we can go any further without defining it. But that's not quite as easy as you might imagine, at least not in a meaningful way. Digital is a slippery fish. It's difficult to get a good grip on it. I remember a conversation with the managing director of a medium-sized business who asked me what I did. I told her that I help leaders of SMEs to adapt their organisations and operating models to become more digital. She looked at me quizzically for a moment and then asked, "What do you mean by digital?"

At first that sounds like a dumb question – but it isn't. It's a very good question indeed. We all think we know what digital is, but defining it in a sentence is difficult. It's one of those words that means different things to different people. We're already more than twenty years into the digital revolution, so we really should know the answer. It's important, because how we define it changes the way we think about it, work with it and explain it to colleagues and other stakeholders. By understanding, really understanding it, hopefully we can all set off in the right direction.

We may feel that we know the answer instinctively. After all, we all feel the effects of digital and know that it has changed our world forever. We know that over the last two decades technology has transformed the way we shop, learn, connect with friends, find recipes, discover new music . . . the list goes on. And we know that this trend will continue into the future.

We also know that it's made the world faster, changing consumer expectations and habits. We are well aware that it's given us more work to do, particularly if we are undertaking digital activities in addition to the analogue stuff we did before. We can't have missed the fact that it's spawned new market entrants with different business and operating models. It is also impossible to deny that it has shifted the balance of power from suppliers to consumers.

But despite those insights, do we really understand it? For example, does "digital" mean the same as "online"? Let's get that out of the way first. Online means that you are connected to the internet. That's it. Digital is more complex. For a start, there is not one agreed definition. In fact, many people who have been working "in digital" for years struggle to articulate a simple meaning (I've asked them).

Literally, according to the *Oxford English Dictionary* it means:

Digital (adjective) (of signals or data) expressed as series of the digits 0 and 1, typically represented by values of a physical quantity such as voltage or magnetic polarization.

But that technical definition doesn't help us much as enterprise leaders. Perhaps the rest of the entry helps:

- relating to, using, or storing data or information in the form of digital signals.
- involving or relating to the use of computer technology.

Hmm . . . data and computers. It sounds like information technology – aka our old friend IT. But it isn't that either. It certainly isn't *just* that.

A popular definition of digital for business is Social, Mobile, Analytics and Cloud – or SMAC for short. This is based on the idea that the convergence of these four applications of digital is currently driving business changes. For me, although useful in highlighting some important aspects, this definition only reveals part of what digital really means in practice.

It also neatly illustrates the challenge of capturing digital's constant evolution in a soundbite, having already been revised as SMACI – that extra "I" added to accommodate the growing impact of the Internet of Things (IoT). It could soon become something like SMACAII to encompass artificial intelligence (AI) or perhaps SMABCAIIVAR to also include Blockchain as well as virtual and augmented reality (VR/AR).

My preferred definition of digital in commercial terms is: "any technology that connects people and machines with information or with each other, facilitating a new way of doing business".

It's fundamentally about *connectivity*. It has created the new connected customer who behaves differently from his analogue ancestors. The combination of technology and tools has changed consumer behaviour. Although it hasn't changed their fundamental wants and needs, the merger of the digital world and what we call "reality" has changed the way consumers see the world.

An understanding of what digital really is matters because it sets the digital agenda within organisations. Depending on their understanding of the definition, some leaders decide that digital is a "customer engagement thing," so they push it over to their marketing people. Others think it's a "technology thing," so they give it to the IT department. But the truth it that digital is not simply a "marketing thing" or an "IT thing". It's a *business thing*" for which there must be shared responsibility across all areas of the organisation. No single function can or should own digital.

Doing versus being

Now that we have a shared understanding of what digital is, let's focus on what it means to leaders and their enterprises. There's a useful distinction to be made between *doing* digital and *being* digital. In a nutshell, doing digital is tactical. But being digital is strategic.

Most organisations have been *doing* digital for so time now. They have been using email for communication, social media to build relationships, search engines to attract prospects and websites to sell to them. When I first started in ecommerce I was *doing* digital. I say that for three reasons. First, as an ecommerce department we were a separate entity, a standalone business function. Second, we were mostly involved in projects that were digitising existing processes and established ways of doing things. Third, the business case was primarily about cost reduction, rather than customer experience enhancement.

There were good reasons for that at the time. We needed to be independent of the existing functional structure of the organisation, reporting directly to the managing director, so that we could focus fully on getting things done, taking an independent perspective on digital priorities, regardless of the impact on other functions. We also needed skill sets, such as web design and programming, content production, direct marketing and customer relationship management that did not already exist within the business. At that time digital business wasn't simply business as usual, and so it couldn't be immediately integrated into the business as usual team.

In order to gain trust and minimise resistance from colleagues so that we could build up change momentum, we initially had to focus on projects that would almost immediately demonstrate a positive return on investment (ROI), without cannibalising existing revenue streams. We were pump-priming, pragmatically doing what we had to do to get the digital ball rolling in the business and secure further investment for the new skills and tools we needed.

In those early days we quickly understood that operating as another siloed department within the organisation wasn't a viable way forward. Everything we did required close collaboration with other functions. We couldn't accurately measure the real return on investment from digital marketing without tracking sales made through our call centre, in addition to the online sales. We couldn't communicate with prospects and turn more of them into customers unless sales staff asked for, and accurately entered, an email address into the database.

We couldn't run an effective digital marketing budget that was flexibly allocated according to the return on the investment data we were getting, without constant negotiation with the finance and marketing departments. We couldn't sell more product online without getting it set-up appropriately by the product department. Although we had our own programmers for the website front end, we couldn't improve our technical infrastructure or integrations with back-end selling systems without petitioning for IT resource. These functions had their own priorities and long-established bureaucracies to negotiate. It all took too long.

We couldn't afford to substantially increase our staff headcount, creating a completely new team of digital experts to backfill a skills deficit in the rest of the business. That is a strategy that many large companies have employed to accelerate digital transformation, but as a medium-sized business it was simply not an option. The change we were trying to make was not the creation of a siloed, two-track business where traditional and digital were in competition with each other. Instead, we wanted the business to fully integrate digital into each and every function – to stop simply *doing* digital and start *being* digital.

Success depended on helping our colleagues to adapt their functions, to see the opportunities and threats, to speed up processes and to build up digital capabilities within their own areas. We had to bring them together to solve problems, persuading departmental heads to designate staff for small, multi-disciplinary project teams.

We had to shift the thinking of IT from a focus on internal functions as their primary customers, to a focus on our *real* customers. That meant finding better processes and embedding digital thinking as a part of the mindset. It was a re-engineering of the business, led by board-level change agents and backed by their leadership team colleagues.

One by one we worked through the issues and overcame the barriers. Increasingly, we started using data to make better and faster decisions, rather than working on guesswork and the HiPPO principle (highest paid person's opinion). We were gradually becoming more joined up, less siloed and more customer focused.

We shared our successes and ensured that everybody knew where we were going and the part they needed to play. After a while, we became a better team, all in the name of digital. That team started to include more machines, as we used the emerging free and subscription tools to help us to automate labour-intensive manual processes and tasks.

It took time, but it worked. Organisational changes were made. For example, the sales and marketing functions were brought together, so that cause and effect was managed and measured effectively. Later, customer service was incorporated. This combination of function, but with a significantly flattened hierarchy, became the customer experience champion, ensuring that every touch point within the customer's journey to purchase and beyond was continually being improved. We were then able to track ROI in a more sophisticated way, measuring our customer acquisition costs against average customer lifetime value, rather than simply based on a one-off transaction.

Why versus how

In many ways I think the most important change was one of mindset. We progressed to asking *why* before *what* or *how*. The power of asking *why* is not, of course, a new idea. The "five whys" is one of the most commonly used process improvement tools, a simple technique that gets to the root cause of a problem so that you can solve the underlying cause. Simon Sinek's book *Start with Why* is a global bestseller based on the simple idea that in business *what* you do matters less than *why* you do it.

A wise friend once said to me that the people who know how work for the people who know why. Remembering to ask "why" is a good habit. As small children we rarely ask *how*, but we constantly ask *why*. You could say that it's our default question – except that we sometimes forget to ask it when we're all grown up.

That is certainly true in the case of digital. It has so many moving parts and moves so quickly that we tend to just ask *how*, often in something of a panic, in our rush to get something, anything, done. For example, the question "*how* can we use Facebook or Twitter" tends to get asked before we have asked *why* we should use them.

We need to know why these digital platforms are relevant to *our* customers first. That will tell us how we should use them for brand awareness, relationship building, customer service or lead generation. It may even lead us to conclude that we should not use them at all, perhaps because they are not as relevant to our target markets as other platforms and we simply don't have the resources to do everything – or at least not everything well.

In the same way, before we ask how to build our new website or app – which content management system we will use and the functionality we will build – we should ask why we are building them. We must start with why it is important in the context of our customers' journey to purchase, and therefore why it is an important part of our overall strategy. Again, answers to the *why* questions will determine how or even *if* we build them. You can apply the same logic to mobile, data and analytics – in fact, any aspect of digital.

We also need to ask strategic why questions such as "why is digital important for the future of our business?" "Why are digital businesses outperforming less digitally savvy competitors?" Once we understand the answers to those questions we can begin to ask the what and how questions.

Questions such as "what implications does digital have for the way we do business now?" "What new opportunities have been created by these changes?" "What threats does this new world pose?" "How can we stay relevant and create more value for our customers within this new ecosystem?" "How do we equip and reorganise ourselves to make it happen?" "What should we prioritise?"

Jeffrey Pfeffer and Robert I. Sutton described something they called the "Knowing-Doing Gap" in a Harvard Business School press article and book in 2000. They asked, "Why do so much education and training, management consulting, and business research and so many books and articles produce so little change in what managers and organizations actually do?"

They weren't specifically addressing digital transformation, but business practices in general. In that context, their answer was that "too many managers want to learn 'how' in terms of detailed practices and techniques, rather than 'why' in terms of philosophy and general guidance for action". In a digital business world that observation is spot on.

Beginning with the question of *how* takes us directly to tactics and implementation before we've done any serious thinking. The question we need to start with is *why*. It is the inspirational element, the glue that binds loosely joined teams together and forms the foundation for the future by getting everybody on the same page. That's important, because although individuals can adapt, it takes a whole organisation to evolve. Asking fundamental questions like "why do we need to change?" and "why do we do things this way?" is the first step a leader can take to achieve team alignment and a shared purpose.

Size matters

Peter Drucker once wrote that "Large organizations cannot be versatile. A large organization is effective through its mass rather than through its agility". That lack of speed and agility provides a huge opportunity for SMEs.

Big business has traditionally had the advantage of access to better technology, but with the advent of the "cloud" and the new tools it has spawned, the technological playing field has been levelled to a great extent. Equally, the huge resources that give big business its power can become its major weakness.

Like an aircraft carrier, large companies suffer from a large tactical diameter. Often the speed with which things get done is inversely proportional to the number of people involved. As soon as you have layers of people involved with their own agendas and egos, things tend to get complicated. That complexity creates multiple weak points, of which groupthink and turf battles are two. In practice that means things get held up or broken.

Big companies, with a few notable exceptions also tend to face the wrong way. Their primary mission is to make money for shareholders, rather than to generate value for customers. This approach, aka maximising shareholder value has been widely condemned. Jack Welch called it "the dumbest idea in the world" in a 2009 interview with the *Financial Times*. He went on to say that "Shareholder value is a result, not a strategy ... your main constituencies are your employees, your customers and your products". But it remains the prevalent context in most large organisations.

This creates a great opportunity for smaller, nimbler organisations, who can effect change faster and with much less investment. Today, there is little to stop them. We now have the technology, and, although smaller teams are seldom perfect, the very fact of being smaller creates a dynamic that is more likely to deliver. Change is simply easier when you have fewer people, less large-scale legacy technology and less hierarchy and bureaucracy – assuming of course that you have people with the right attitude and skills.

That's why larger organisations are beginning to shift to a more agile way of working. They have understood that change tends to be faster and more successful when smaller, cross-functional teams are deployed. Leaders of large enterprises know that in a time of major disruption, such as the industrial or digital revolutions, it is those who fail to get the innovation balance right who end up losing their shirts and clearing their desks.

So, many leaders have spent the last decade taking their organisations on a journey to digital fitness. They have been asking those hard *why* questions and taking action based on their findings, in the process that has become known as "digital transformation". This process has become a global industry in its own right, one that has doubled in size to a reported $44 billion in consultancy fees alone for 2017. Big business has the resources to get help and the giant management consultancies have quickly mobilised themselves to take advantage of that need and those resources. In contrast, few SMEs do. They have to be more self-reliant.

Consequently, while big businesses have been cracking on with their programmes of digital transformation, many SMEs, although by no means all, have been sitting on their hands. Consequently, they need to guard against becoming the squeezed middle, caught between new entrants who start from a digital-first mindset and the larger organisations who have invested heavily in getting their digital business act together.

Added to that, some established SMEs are facing a triple whammy of their old adversaries aggressively retooling and re-engineering for their digital future, in addition to the threat from new competitors and the behemoths.

Digital transformation?

[Digital transformation: the change associated with the application of digital technology in all aspects of human society. ... The transformation stage means that digital usages inherently enable new types of innovation and creativity in a particular domain, rather than simply enhance and support traditional methods.]

This definition of digital transformation from Wikipedia contains five key words. Two of them are *digital technology*. Three others are more important, and they are *human, innovation* and *creativity*.

Digital transformation, or more accurately "business transformation", is a response to the rapid adoption by humans (customers) of digital technology powered by the internet. Transformation success depends upon humans (employees) working effectively with digital technology to deliver better customer experiences for other humans.

It enables new ways of working and creating value (innovation) rather than simply enhancing traditional methods. It frees humans to do what they are best at (creativity) while the machines do more of the heavy lifting. Once fit for digital, your business becomes a harmonious collaboration between humans and machines. It becomes bionic; better than it was before; better, stronger, faster.

Survival of the fittest

[Fitness: The condition of being physically fit and healthy. *Biology* An organism's ability to survive and reproduce in a particular environment. Synonyms: suitability, capability, competency, proficiency, ability, aptitude.]

Nothing lasts forever. Organisations come and go, of course. The only constant is change. But over the last fifty years, the average lifespan of companies has shrunk from sixty to under twenty years.

The market is the final arbiter of success, but I'm not sure that all the casualties are fundamentally bad businesses. No doubt many are and their loss is mourned only by the employees and their creditors. But I think perhaps there are many more that have simply fallen out of step with the modern business world, left behind by smarter, more nimble competitors. They have simply lost their relevance to the modern connected consumer.

For many enterprises, getting fit for digital is really about survival. The sense of urgency for change is usually a function of how close the prospect of extinction appears to be. The most motivated companies tend to be those who can clearly see the writing writ large on the wall. Perhaps they have already been disrupted by new market entrants or competitors who have successfully re-engineered themselves. Standing on the proverbial burning deck can really focus the mind.

For the most successful businesses, of course, there is less incentive to explore fundamental change. It's easier to find the resources but harder to find the will. The temptation is to adapt, with fragmented technology projects paid for from departmental budgets, rather than evolve with a centrally budgeted, integrated strategy driven from the top.

It's the digital sideshow versus digital as the main event. But, as John F. Kennedy famously put it, "the time to repair the roof is when the sun is shining". Businesses should look to disrupt themselves before others do it for them and they become the wounded impala of the business savannah.

For many organisations, the extinction clock is ticking. The invasive bionic businesses are multiplying, often cherry-picking the most profitable parts of a business, leaving incumbents with the commercial consolation prize. With their streamlined operating models and business superpowers, they are becoming pervasive.

Native species, those organisations who fail to evolve, risk being decimated. Many are already drifting towards that "red list" of endangered businesses. Tony Robbins said, "Change happens when the pain of staying the same is greater than the pain of change". In an increasingly digital world that may be too late.

The International Union for Conservation of Nature has compiled a Red List of Threatened Species. The organisation describes the inventory as a warning flag, signalling for global attention the perilous status of many species. They have been disrupted, their habitats destroyed or taken over by invasive species forcing them into an existential fight for survival. Maybe there should also be a red list for businesses. Maybe somewhere there is.

[Invasive species: any kind of living organism that is not native to an ecosystem and which causes harm.]

It may not be comfortable, but it is worth reflecting on the threats posed by new market entrants. These "invasive species" can be very harmful to your market share, revenue and profits. These businesses are already among us, and not just the digital superpowers like Amazon or Google.

The barriers to market entry in many industries has been dramatically lowered by the internet and the new business models it supports. This new species of business probably doesn't look, think or act like yours. They don't have traditional hierarchies or operate in functional silos.

They don't have legacy systems that slow down innovation. Sometimes they don't even have desks, as remote workers are empowered to be productive wherever they are. They are digitally fit and bionic. They have begun to harness technology in a way that integrates seamlessly with the humans – their people and their customers – creating a significant competitive advantage for themselves.

[Bionic: utilising electronic devices and mechanical parts to assist humans in performing difficult, dangerous, or intricate tasks.]

Bionic businesses have recognised that the new digital technology sitting in the cloud and accessed through the web changes everything, just as the invention of power, first in the form of steam and then electricity, fundamentally changed the way things were done in a superpowered, new world of mass production.

A good example is the technology-driven US insurer, Lemonade. The company offers renters and home owners insurance products promising "zero paperwork and instant everything by replacing brokers and bureaucracy with bots and machine learning". It enables customers who have lost property to submit claims via a video message on their mobile phones. Claims are reviewed using anti-fraud algorithms and, if everything checks out, the appropriate funds can be transferred to the customer's bank account in, it claims, a matter of seconds.

Most established organisations have yet to collectively make that mental and cultural leap. They have struggled to move from a mindset of thinking of digital technology as a communication tool or something that can make their business as usual more efficient, to an understanding that it changes what business as usual activity actually *is*.

So, what are these bionic superpowers? Here are just a few examples:

- *Super hearing*: when you can use social listening software to overhear what people are saying and track sentiment about your business even when you're not in the room. Or use "the power of the crowd" for funding or to prioritise product enhancements based on customer collaboration, allowing your community to vote, rate, and rank suggested changes.

- *Super speed*: when you can use data to make fast and informed decisions and act on them quickly using digital technology, team collaboration and agile processes.

- *Super strength and stamina*: using technology to automate repetitive tasks in the office or factory and help each person to do the work of many, thus freeing up their time to add value in other ways which are more interesting and rewarding for them, their customers and the company.

- *Super service*: when you can sensitively anticipate the next move of a prospect or customer based on what content they've looked at, what products they have previously purchased and where they are in the buying process.

- *Super selling*: when you can target prospects much more precisely using social media profiling or use free tools to gauge demand in terms of keyword searches. Or when you use analytics software to see exactly what people are doing and in what numbers on your website or app.

[Artificial intelligence or AI: the development of computer systems able to perform tasks normally requiring human intelligence, such as visual perception, speech recognition, decision-making and translation between languages.]

Artificial intelligence is making speedy progress in acquiring skills that were previously regarded as exclusively human. AI, in the form of IBM's chess-playing computer, Deep Blue, beat the grandmaster Gary Kasparov over two decades ago. That was quite a feat, as it's estimated that there are more possible iterations of a game of chess than there are atoms in the known universe. And AI has come on a bit since then. It's the next big thing in our digital and social evolution, and is already playing an increasing role in our everyday lives, from serving up search engine results, helping us to navigate our cars, suggesting entertainment options, making shopping recommendations and automating more and more jobs.

There are two main flavours in the application of AI. The first, known as "classical AI", involves applications powered by algorithms, which are essentially a set of rules given to them by humans that allows them to take decisions. This works best in a controlled environment such as a factory, a microcosm where everything is ordered and controlled, but struggles in the chaos and almost infinite variability of the "real" world. The second flavour, "machine learning", copes better with messiness. Instead of giving computers the rules, machine learning lets them figure out solutions on their own from raw data. The more data they have, the better they can perform.

Many of us are now interacting with AI when we use online customer service. Large businesses are adopting chatbots to deal with routine customer questions and tasks 24/7. You may well have already "talked" to one of these virtual assistants when using the online chat functions offered by more and more companies. Increasingly, they are being used to direct and support online shoppers in making purchase decisions.

Big business is beginning to grasp the opportunity which AI offers to reduce the cost of their workforce, saving human employees for more challenging, higher-revenue-earning tasks. For example, if your flight is cancelled, a chatbot can leap into action and offer you the next available flight, which is considerably more useful than a text or email alert simply telling you that you won't be travelling as planned.

AI has already replaced humans in some situations. "Edward", the "virtual host" at several Radisson Blu hotels, is able to tell guests about hotel amenities, provide other information, check guests in and deal with some complaints. "He" is so convincing, according to Radisson Blu, that more than 90 per cent of guests think he is human, responding with thanks and sometimes even the offer of tips.

Robo-advisers have also become the latest trend in the world of personal financial advice. These computer programs use algorithms to create smart, diversified investment plans. They're easy to use, inexpensive and increasingly popular. Just as technology helps us to call a cab or watch television, when and where we like, personalised technology is now bringing financial planning to the masses.

As the Alexas and Siris of the modern world gain sophistication and acceptance, it's just a matter of time before we all have personal AI assistants to tend to our diaries and desires. In fact, AI today is most visible in devices such as Amazon Echo, Google Home and Apple HomePod, which have already been installed in millions of homes worldwide. Applications like self-driving cars, smart home security systems and intelligent refrigerators are also changing our understanding of what's possible.

These virtual assistants will soon make it into our offices, providing the opportunity to boost productivity and automate more of the repetitive tasks that suck in resources and waste our time. Few SMEs are in a position to develop customised AI applications themselves, but a raft of new applications for such enterprises are being developed by vendors. As natural language voice interfaces improve further, the take up of such systems will accelerate. We will, for example, soon see more businesses using AI to collate and present actionable data that can be used by anyone in the organisation.

Despite these impressive applications, AI is in many ways still in its infancy. It has its limitations and there are many issues that have yet to be ironed out. The machines may have long ago surpassed human logical thinking, but they still lack what we could characterise as "common sense". They tend to miss the subtleties of language and intonation and struggle to deal with unpredictable situations. As a result, most AI-powered bots are still supervised by humans.

There is, of course, widespread concern that the machines will make humans redundant in the workplace. I tend to side with those who think that humans will not be consigned to the scrapheap just yet. No one can be sure, but on the evidence of previous industrial revolutions, that seems unlikely, at least in the short term. As with similar seismic events, the likely outcome is that more jobs will be created, but with humans performing different roles. As Erik Brynjolfsson and Andrew Mcafee put it: "Over the next decade, artificial intelligence won't replace managers, but managers who use AI will replace those who don't".

Bibliography

Anthony, Scott D. (2012) How to Anticipate a Burning Platform (11 December). Available at https://hbr.org/2012/12/how-to-anticipate-a-burning-platform.

Brynjolfsson, Erik and Mcafee, Andrew (2017) The Business of Artificial Intelligence. Available at https://hbr.org/cover-story/2017/07/the-business-of-artificial-intelligence (accessed 4 March 2018).

Burns, Janet (2016) Radisson Blu Edwardian Guests Can Now Text Edward the Chatbot For Service. Available at https://www.forbes.com/sites/janetwburns/2016/05/10/radisson-blu-hotelguests-can-now-text-edward-the-chatbot-for-service/#63914f021e23 (accessed 5 March 2018).

Chatbots (n.d.) Available at https://en.wikipedia.org/wiki/Chatbot (accessed 8 March 2018).

Consultancy.uk (2018) Digital Transformation Consulting Market Accelerates to $44 Billion (22 May). Available at www.consultancy.uk/news/17223/digital-transformation-consulting-market-accelerates-to-44-billion (accessed 13 June 2018).

Crook, Jordan (2016) Lemonade Wants to Rewrite the Insurance Policy Itself (22 May). Available at https://techcrunch.com/2018/05/16/lemonade-wants-to-rewrite-the-insurance-policy-itself/ (accessed 23 May 2018).

Davenport, Thomas H. (2018) Robo-Advisers Are Coming to Consulting and Corporate Strategy. Available at https://hbr.org/2018/01/robo-advisers-are-coming-to-consulting-andcorporate-strategy (accessed 24 March 2018).

Denning, Steve (2011) The Dumbest Idea in The World: Maximizing Shareholder Value. Available at www.forbes.com/sites/stevedenning/2011/11/28/maximizing-shareholder value-the-dumbest-idea-in-the-world/2/#27b0b6de1e38 (accessed 16 November 2017).

Five Whys (n.d.). Available at https://en.wikipedia.org/wiki/5_Whys (accessed 4 January 2018).

Kennedy, John F. (1962) Annual Message to the Congress on the State of the Union (7) (11 January). Available at www.jfklibrary.org/asset-viewer/archives/JFKPOF/037/JFKPOF-037-004 (accessed 6 March 2018).

Koetsier, John. (2018) AI Assistants Ranked: Google's Smartest, Alexa's Catching Up, Cortana Surprises, Siri Falls Behind (24 April). Available at www.forbes.com/sites/johnkoetsier/2018/04/24/ai-assistants-ranked-googles-smartest-alexas-catching-up-cortana-surprises-siri-falls-behind/#170dd47a492a (accessed 4 March 2018).

Kübler-Ross, E. (2014) On Death and Dying: What the Dying Have to Teach Doctors, Nurses, Clergy and their Own Families. New York: Scribner.

Levy, Steven. (2017) What Deep Blue Tells Us about AI (May). Available at www.wired.com/2017/05/what-deep-blue-tells-us-about-ai-in-2017/ (accessed 18 February 2018).

Pfeffer, J. (2010) The Knowing-Doing Gap. Hamilton: Summaries.com.

Red List (2013) Available at www.iucnredlist.org/ (accessed 5 March 2018).

Rouse, Margaret (2014) SMAC (Social, Mobile, Analytics and Cloud) (29 July). Available at: https://searchcio.techtarget.com/definition/SMAC-social-mobile-analytics-and-cloud (accessed 14 March 2018).

Sheetz, Michael (2018). CNBC (15 May). Available at www.cnbc.com/2017/08/24/technology-killing-off-corporations-average-lifespan-of-company-under-20-years.html (accessed 24 March 2018).

Silverberg, David (2017) Why You Need to Question Your Hippo Boss (20 April). Available at www.bbc.co.uk/news/business-39633499 (accessed 3 March 2018).

Trout, Jack (2006) Peter Drucker on Marketing. Available at www.forbes.com/2006/06/30/Jack-Trout-On-MarketingCx_Jt_0703drucker.Html#8debf05555cb (accessed 16 January 2018).

Part 2

The process

Six steps to get fit for digital business

When it's a matter of the survival of the fittest, it makes sense to get fit. In fact, there is a close analogy between digital transformation and the process of getting *physically* fit. You start with a commitment to change, usually inspired by a moment of truth. Then you assess where you're starting from, identifying the areas you need to work on. Next you create a vivid mental picture of what you're aiming to become, before creating an integrated programme to make it happen.

In essence it's as simple as that. But, because shifting from *doing* digital to *being* digital is more about people than tech, leaders need a strong narrative to get everyone and everything pulling in the same direction. It helps to have a change story that can be communicated effectively and engagingly to a whole team, some of whom will no doubt have a healthy scepticism towards what they perceive to be management bullshit.

Getting fit for digital business is the narrative I have developed. It starts with a clear six-step process (see Figure 1), so that everybody knows the way the programme will play out, and focuses on the six key components of digital business fitness. Let's start with the process.

Figure 1 Get fit for digital business process

Step 1: Owning the moment of truth

As the psychotherapist and writer Nathaniel Branden observed, "The first step towards change is awareness". That awareness often comes in a flash of clarity and inspiration. In other words, a moment of truth.

[Moment of truth: when you are struck by a crucial insight and must make a decision that will have important consequences in the future.]

I'm writing this in January. Traditionally, this is the time of year when we resolve to make changes in our lives. We tell ourselves that this will be the year when we eat better, perhaps drink less alcohol and generally get into shape. We make resolutions because we want to be better versions of ourselves. We know we should change our habits. We know this will help us to feel and perform better. We want to be stronger, more energised and agile. But despite these good intentions many of us fail to put them into effect.

Usually there are no immediate consequences. We say to ourselves, OK, so we are carrying a bit of extra weight, have some aches and pains and generally feel a bit lacking in "oomph". But we are still functioning and getting through the days, right? But behind the bravado, somewhere in the back of our minds, is that niggling thought that through our inactivity we're simply storing up trouble for ourselves down the line.

So, what's stopping us from doing something about this? Perhaps it's just that life gets in the way and we don't get enough support to make changes and stick with them. Perhaps we're unsure where to start and how to go about it. We might understandably be concerned about doing ourselves an injury and getting into worse shape than we were before. Or maybe we're just plain lazy and can't be bothered to get off the sofa.

Well, those could all be factors for most of us. But in the end it boils down to motivation and commitment. Ask any personal trainer. If you do, they'll say that you need clear targets, good planning and ideally a workout programme that you will actually enjoy. Most of all you need the will to succeed.

Without that, it's almost impossible to maintain the commitment or energy required to achieve your goals. It's only when you persevere that you begin to see results. That's when good habits become ingrained into your everyday life, a muscle memory that begins to feel natural. Typically, that commitment is driven by a moment of truth, a decisive moment when something clicks in your head and you decide, *really* decide, to act – because you know it's important to your future.

For you personally this moment of truth could be anything from a bad hangover to a serious health scare. Or even just a look at yourself in the bathroom mirror. It could be a simple realisation that if you want to continue to feel good and perform well as you mature, you need to start getting into better shape. Whatever it is, it becomes the trigger for commitment and the fuel for motivation.

And you need that, because once you've started you have to keep going to ensure that you don't lose the gains you've made. After all, it's not unusual to join the gym in January but stop going by March. We have good intentions but somehow our resolve weakens and the best-laid plans get derailed.

It's the same with business. It can be tough to find the time to effect *real* change. But we need to make the time; it boils down to good planning coupled with real commitment.

Like getting physically fit, there's no silver bullet – no magic technology or tool – that will effortlessly transform the weak into the strong and the slow into the fast. Ultimately, it's about the will of the leadership team to effect deep and meaningful change because they have understood that there is no alternative. They have reached a moment of truth and have collectively decided to own it.

For some that moment of truth is a simple realisation that they need to go deeper with digital. For these business leaders, it's a proactive, offensive change. Typically, such companies are already keeping up but want to accelerate growth by making better use of digital channels and technology. For others, it's more defensive, a response to a business platform that is already on fire due to new customer demands, or new digitally focused market entrants or established competitors who have got their digital business act together.

Some leaders have spotted an opportunity to disrupt the market with a new product and/or business model. These are the market-making companies that look for new ways of selling, rather than waiting for their existing business platforms to smoulder.

In my experience, every transformation starts from a moment of truth, which in turn leads to an honest assessment of the gap between where you are now and where you need to be. Only then are leaders fully prepared and emotionally ready to commit to making meaningful change happen.

As personal trainers insist on saying, you won't get the ass you want by sitting on it.

Step 2: The fitness assessment

The objective of a digital fitness assessment is to get a shared understanding of the current digital capability of your people, processes and platforms. It reveals and articulates your strengths, weaknesses, opportunities and threats, and identifies ways of filling the capability gaps. It is one part of the fitness journey where some external help will be useful to assess the shape you are in, benchmarked by comparison with the traditional competitors and new entrants in your market.

You will need an independent perspective and someone to help you to ask the right questions and tell you the things you don't know that you don't know. Think of the assessment as a digital maturity fact-base, the foundation for the creation of your digital business vision. Or, if you prefer a different emphasis, your new business vision in the context of digital.

Many organisations plough ahead without advice from independent specialists in the field, something they are unlikely to do with other key business areas such taxation or law. Many digital agencies aren't equipped to help. Often, they are in the business of selling you the services they have capability in, rather than helping you to build the internal capability that is essential to the creation of a truly digital business. But flying solo is also a risky way forward. Making the wrong decisions can prove costly in terms of time and money, particularly when they are in the high-spend areas – people, systems and marketing – that are so impacted by digital.

The assessment is effectively a change initiation plan, setting out priorities, identifying quick wins and the longer-term action required. When you know where you are and where you want to be, you can then set specific goals. These become the heart of the business case for change, highlighting the financial and other resources required, and where they're coming from – for example redirected from less productive or outdated activities – and most importantly, the projected return on investment.

So, once you've committed to make change happen, do an assessment and have your vital signs checked. It can help to prevent a business version of a coronary.

Need-to-know workout tips: ten fitness assessment areas of focus

1   Overall and digital business objectives.
2   Distribution channels and supply chain digitisation opportunities.
3   Current digital approach – strategy, skills, structure and resources; cross-functional collaboration.
4   Current customers, target audience and customer experience analysis.

5 Use of data and analytics; current key performance indicators (KPIs) and online performance review.
6 Budgeting flexibility and allocation.
7 Digital marketing; content, customer relationship management (CRM), search marketing, online advertising, mobile and social media.
8 Technology platforms and infrastructure.
9 Web development and approach to technology evolution.
10 Testing and optimisation strategy and tactics.

Step 3: Visualisation

An important aspect of getting yourself physically fit is visualisation; motivating yourself by imagining how you will look and feel when you've got in shape. In the same way, digital provides the opportunity to reimagine a rebooted business. It's important to be clear about where you are leading your team, so your vision should vividly paint the big picture of the organisation, culturally and operationally, as it would look in a future successful state. In other words, a good vision is the answer to the question: "if the organisation were to achieve all of its strategic goals to thrive within a digital marketplace, what would it look like five years from now?"

It provides the context to look again at your business model, question the way you market and position yourself; to think about your customers' experience, how you want the business to grow and feel culturally and operationally. I must admit that early in my career I made the mistake of dismissing the value of a vision. I had "proper" work to do. The fluffy stuff could wait.

But I was wrong. In fact, in a digital world in which you must provide consistent messages across a myriad of channels, and get a diverse group of people working more effectively together, a compelling vision is more important than ever. A strong vision is part of the foundation for change; if you skimp on those foundations you're going get subsidence and that's always expensive to put right.

A fuzzy vision inevitably leads to a shapeless strategy, resulting in a myriad of different interpretations across the business. In turn, that leads to a loss of alignment and poor outcomes. On the other hand, an effective vision guides us, giving us a clear sense of purpose and helps to build a consensus on digital business objectives across the organisation.

In the course of my consultancy work, I've noticed that painting an inspiring picture of the enterprise's future goals and aspirations is a low priority for many leaders. Some of my clients have said that they already have a vision statement, but that everybody finds it a bit of a joke. If that's the case, then there's a good chance that it is an uninspiring piece of corporate speak or that it has simply lost its relevance in a digital world. My advice is to look at it again through a digital lens. It doesn't matter what sort of organisation you lead, nor its size. No business is too small to have a vision.

Leaders should set the agenda but they must also engage people at all levels within the company in order to bring the vision alive. Everybody in an organisation needs to participate, to contribute to and understand the why, what and how of your digital business ambition. Yes, there may be aspects that require commercial confidentiality for a variety of reasons. But as a general principle, your team should be crystal clear about where the company is heading. The team at Amazon can be in little doubt about where they headed: "Our vision is to be earth's most customer centric company;

to build a place where people can come to find and discover anything they might want to buy online".

That's a very clear vision that will send shivers down the spine of many business leaders. If you haven't defined your overall change vision, your digital transformation will be limited in its impact and relevance to the wider team.

Your vision is of course neither your mission, nor your values statement. Each has its own distinct role to play in the strategic planning process. (I'll cover mission and values statements in Part 3, when we'll look at why they too are more important than ever in a connected world.) None of this requires an army of brand consultants for SMEs. You should be able to reach consensus based on the fitness assessment findings and some facilitated sessions that focus everyone on the key issues.

Your digital future vision should not be carved in stone. It can and should evolve over time, as the capabilities of your people and technologies advance. For example, Procter & Gamble started with a vision to become completely digitised. But later this vision evolved to reflect an ambition to become a real-time operating and decision-making environment *powered* by digital – a subtle but powerful change in emphasis.

Almost a decade ago now, Burberry led the fashion industry with its vision statement:

> We have a vision – to be the first company that is fully digital end-to-end . . . The experience is that the customer will have total access to Burberry across any device, anywhere . . . they will get exactly the same feeling of the brand, feeling of the culture, regardless of where, when and how they were accessing . . . totally connected with everyone who touches [our] brand.

Burberry has focused on the implementation of a more integrated customer experience through digital channels, working to seamlessly blur the lines between physical and digital.

It can also help to create a vision statement that places some tangible goals within it. These measures should be very high level as they will be fleshed out in the organisation's specific, measurable, achievable, realistic and timebound (SMART) objectives. For example:

- We will be number one in terms of digital audience share in our market segment in [*insert territory*] by [*insert date*].
- By [*insert date*] X per cent of total sales will be digitally generated.
- By [*insert date*] Y per cent of our customers will love our digital services and will recommend them to a friend.
- Two out of three customer service contacts will be digital by [*insert date*].

This combination of intent and outcome gives everyone in the organisation a clear set of guidelines to help them to envision new ways of working. It also ensures that the focus of the transformative vision is not on the technology itself, but on different ways of operating, identifying new ways to improve performance and customer satisfaction.

We'll get into setting SMART objectives a little later. But first let's take a look at the digital transformation options you need to consider. As a leader, you will need to be clear about the sort of transformation you want to achieve, so that the wider team trusts the direction of travel and stays on side. It shouldn't be assumed that everybody thinks of digital transformation in the same way.

For instance, one person in the leadership team may define digital transformation as a complete re-engineering of the *business* model, based on digital technology. Much of the discussion about digital transformation has tended to focus on business models. Headlines about entirely new business models, such as the sharing economy, where consumers engage in peer-to-peer exchanging of products and services, are sexier than stories of digitised *operating* models.

A business model essentially describes the way in which a business captures value. For example, when a manufacturer designs and produces a product, its aim is to create something that is considerably more valuable than the raw materials that are the sum of its parts. If it succeeds it has captured value.

[Target operating model: a high-level representation of how a company can be best organised to more efficiently and effectively deliver and execute its strategy.]

Some members of a leadership team may be more focused on the operating model. In simple terms the operating model is the combination and formation of people, processes and technology used to power the business model. Other members may be thinking of digital transformation in terms of specific elements of the operating model, such as improving customer experience or operations. There is nothing wrong with that, as long as everybody understands that each element is just part of a digital transformation, and that the real value is generated when all the key elements come together.

Often leaders think in terms of a digital *upgrade* rather than a transformation. In truth, most companies aim to achieve digital transformation but end up with digital upgrades, using digital technology to increase the efficiency or effectiveness of something they are already doing. For example, they might increase their marketing spend on digital channels, upgrade internal communication systems or build a new website.

Digital *transformation* is only achieved when you use digital technology to change the way you operate, particularly in terms of customer interaction and the way that value is created. If you discover that you are actually embarking on an upgrade instead of a transformation, ask yourself if that will be sufficient to maintain competitiveness in the years to come. Let's take a look at a few examples of different digital transformation approaches and emphasis.

Boeing has been focusing its digital efforts on achieving operational excellence. It is working to improve performance by using AI and advanced analytics to better predict aircraft maintenance requirements, optimise fuel use, improve systems and the passenger onboard experience. It is committed to the creation of a more seamless and transparent supply chain to encourage closer collaboration with suppliers and to increase the speed of decision making based on hard data.

The LEGO Group uses digital to better understand its customers by encouraging them to co-create products through its LEGO® IDEAS online community. If a proposed idea gets 10,000 votes, it is reviewed by LEGO and may be manufactured and sold globally. The creator earns a percentage of any sales generated and gets recognition as the creator on all packaging.

Perhaps the most pertinent example for our digital fitness theme is Under Armour. This US company has undergone a deep transformation from a shirts and shoes company into the world's largest digital connected fitness company. Through acquisitions such as MapMyFitness, EndoMondo and MyFitnessPal as well as new product launches such as UA Record, it has become the largest digital fitness community in the world, with a growing membership of over 200 million worldwide. The company has forged direct relationships with a vast and receptive audience on all seven continents, exposing its brand as integral to the idea of improving the lives of all athletes, both professional and amateur.

Under Armour has also begun to incorporate tracking technology into its apparel products that automatically track your health and fitness activity, syncing with apps so that you can leave your phone at home. It is fully integrating its physical products directly into the digital experience, and in the process creating extremely valuable data. The company's objective is a single customer view, whereby retail transactions are linked with the connected fitness data.

That data and the insights derived from this process will enable Under Armour to offer highly personalised and contextually relevant consumer experiences and improve the alignment of its product innovations to the way in which consumers actually use them. In practice, this means that Under Armour staff can use an iPad to access the data and determine by sport or activity the profile and gender mix in any defined location. This should help the company to design better products and to connect with its audience segments more effectively.

None of the above-mentioned businesses are SMEs, of course. But the principle of thinking differently about the creation of value is the same for any almost every scale of business. Digital transformations come in a variety of flavours, but none of them has to be mutually exclusive. The important thing for SMEs is to take it step by step, in the context of an overall get fit for digital roadmap, so that the humans can keep up, while getting the day job done.

Need-to-know workout tips: eight benefits of an effective vision statement

A good vision is the answer to the question: "if the organisation were to achieve all of its strategic goals, what would it look like five years from now?"

1   Paints a mental image of the future state of the organisation, giving purpose and meaning to what everybody does.
2   Links vision to high-level future objectives.
3   Is inspirational, aspirational, challenging and energising – yet simple and memorable.
4   Appropriate for both internal and external audiences, including employees, partners, board members, customers and shareholders.
5   Shows how you will use digital to improve the customer experience.
6   Shows the benefit to the business if you innovate and invest in digital, in terms of growth, operational efficiency and profitability.
7   Helps to drive endurance, providing motivation to stick with a programme of change.
8   Facilitates focus and prioritisation in order to keep the main things front of mind and stay focused on the 20 per cent of activities that really matter.

Step 4: Warming up

Assuming you now have the bit between your teeth, it's time to get the organisation warmed up and ready to start your digital fitness workout programme. Some loosening up will reduce the chance of triggering the stresses and strains that often impede progress. Think of your team as muscles that need stretching in order to improve their flexibility, increase blood flow and reduce resistance.

If you don't get your people to buy in, they won't weigh in and get behind a programme of change. An organisation needs to be readied psychologically before activity begins in earnest. Getting fit for digital relies on the actions of multiple employees working together in a coordinated manner. Each one of them must assess and alter their existing habits to support the organisation's change goals.

Demanding change just doesn't work. People rarely change their thinking and behaviour simply because they are told to do so. Time and effort spent on preparing for change will make the difference between success and failure, because the real challenge of effecting change is human rather than technological. The team must understand the reasons why their culture and ways of working have to change, what the changes will actually look like and their individual role in making it happen.

Unlike modern software, we humans are hard to update and can only handle so much change at once. The machines we have today don't feel. They don't care who they work with or how they are put to work. They don't crave meaning or power – at least not yet. But people care quite a lot. Sure, systems can break under strain; that's why we stress-test them. But stress-testing our people with lots of change for which they are underprepared is not going to bring about a happy outcome.

Inevitably, as a leader of change you will need to overcome some resistance from your own people. Not everyone likes change. In fact, few of us do, often for very rational reasons. At the root of this resistance is fear. Fear of losing control. Fear of losing one's job. Fear of losing commission. Change brings uncertainty. That's inevitable and unavoidable.

But there is much that leaders can do to mitigate such fear. It can be tempting to see resistance to change as simply a bump in the road and to look for a quick route around or over it. But it is important to confront the issues, understand why your team might be resistant to change and to address the people factors from the outset.

Let's not sugar-coat this. There are people who seem to resist any and every plan for change. We've all had the pleasure of working with them. They are set in their ways, are sometimes disruptive and will fight any change tooth and nail, regardless of whether it is potentially beneficial to them and for the good of the organisation. They are not the kind of people who read books like this, so I think I'm pretty safe to call them out. The bottom line with refuseniks is that they will continue to operate in that way for as long as the organisation allows them to.

But in my experience, these people are very much in the minority. Fortunately, most people don't resist change just to be awkward. They're just busy, fully focused on their tasks and deadlines. They don't often get the chance to take a breath, put up their periscopes and look at the horizon. Change is disruptive and uncomfortable, and a distraction from the day job. It can be tricky to tell everyone to fix what's perceived as unbroken.

We all get set in our ways to some extent. When tasks become habitual they take considerably less mental energy to perform. They effectively become hardwired, requiring little conscious effort. Doing things the way we've always done them just feels right, which is why logic and common sense don't always win the day when you are pitching for change.

It helps to remember that resistance to change is actually pretty rational and normal. This is partly because our brains are hardwired (the neuronal reasons); partly because of our psychological needs; partly due to our sociological needs; and partly because we may dislike the practical effect a change might have on us. Sometimes opposition is not about the ultimate goal; it may just be unhappiness about the process of getting there.

In a business environment, the fear of change is often a learned behaviour; namely, the result of being previously involved in change that has been poorly thought through and shoddily implemented. It's worth casting your mind back to any change programmes you have been involved in or heard about. Perhaps some of these factors will ring some bells in your memory:

- The change planning was poor or non-existent.
- The change was poorly communicated or not communicated at all.
- Key staff were not consulted about the change.
- The timing of the change was poor.
- Timescales were unrealistic.
- Outcomes were unrealistic.
- Change tasks were piled onto existing workloads. The people charged with making the change were not backfilled or given latitude on their standard business-as-usual tasks in order to offset the extra effort required to implement the change.
- Generally, insufficient resources were allocated to support a successful change process.
- The "right" people were not held accountable for making the change successful.

- Once implemented, the change resulted in more work than the process it replaced.
- Aspects of the outcome were negative, e.g. redundancies; inappropriate reassignments; a mass exodus of good employees; the promotion of the "wrong" people.

Many people's experience of change tells them that they will feel some pain before they start feeling the benefits – assuming they feel any benefits at all. So, it's perfectly rational for people to feel "once bitten, twice shy".

We humans are pretty complex creatures. In order to buy into change we have to be convinced, rationally and emotionally, that it will bring real benefits to the team and to ourselves. Fear will always be present. The future doesn't come with guarantees. It's natural to question whether the reality of the changed future will really feel better than the tried and tested past. It's a risk, and the certainty of the present, with all its downsides and frustrations, may trump the desire to move forward.

In addition, up until now digital has arguably done more to increase pressure than alleviate it. It has forced us all to respond faster and do more. This has been particularly the case as businesses go through a period of double-tasking – doing the old analogue stuff as well as the new digital tasks. Just think about what a marketing team used to do and what they do (or could do) now.

In some organisations people feel overwhelmed by digital. Often, they need to be persuaded that working with tech will make life easier for them, not harder, and that their jobs can become more rewarding. They need to know what's in it for them. During the implementation phase it's vital to give training to help to make employees comfortable with the technology and to ensure that they are actually using it to the full. Only then will it make their lives better as well as improving their performance.

Of course, there's also the fundamental fear of losing your job. Many business cases have been made to boards pitching digital as a short cut to cost reductions, usually in print and people. That has made people understandably wary. But the truth is that so far digital has actually created jobs because companies have been able to set themselves up digitally and expand faster nationally and internationally. However, employees are often placed in different roles and some skills development is usually required.

There will also be some wariness, even hostility, towards the potential implications for established authority and power bases, even within relatively small organisations. The human organism tends not to give up its resources willingly or without a fight. Even positive changes can cause stress, because they're taking us out of established patterns of behaviour into the unknown. Again, that's why any digital transformation must be a people-first programme rather than a digital technology-first initiative.

That is probably the biggest lesson I have learnt in my personal journey through digital business so far. While I thought I was simply schooling myself about digital platforms, tools and techniques in business, I was actually learning more about how people individually and collectively react to the challenge of change. The "get fit for digital business" metaphor, while hopefully a little more engaging than management consultancy speak, also has a more serious side to it. It helps to address one of the challenges we continue to face on our personal digital business journeys.

That challenge is that people find it difficult to imagine the future. We humans usually think about things in increments, often in isolation from the bigger picture. We tend to get into individual projects – such as a website redesign – before standing back to understand the role our website plays in our overall strategy.

Businesses often shy away from change due to the perception of risk or fear of the expense of transition. But these concerns can be addressed by the right approach, such as managing costs and risks with a transition plan and spending smarter rather than spending more. As a guiding principle then, effort spent in getting your people properly warmed up for change is always a worthwhile investment.

In practice, warming up a team to get fit for digital is primarily about mindset. Therefore, SME leaders need to get their people "in the zone" and understand how to overcome resistance – the biggest blocker of digital transformation. I'll cover this in greater depth in Part 3.

Step 5: The digital fitness roadmap

Once you know where you going, and everybody is sufficiently warmed up, you need to plot your route to get there. That's where the roadmap comes in. A good roadmap brings everything together in a visual representation of goals, timelines and intermediate stops on your journey to digital fitness. It is a statement of consensus about priorities and the holistic plan of action to get fit for digital. It should provide a realistic blueprint for execution, helping teams to navigate obstacles and make decisions as conditions dictate.

In fact, rather than an old school roadmap, I prefer to think of it as satellite navigation, directing you on the fastest route to your destination. It must also reflect the interdependencies of the milestones, and, like sat nav, help you to plan alternative routes if you meet heavy traffic or roadblocks along the way. Roadmaps are not static tools and need to be regularly reviewed to evaluate progress and make any necessary changes in approach when moving forward.

The process of creating a roadmap must be collaborative, based on the assumption that different functional areas in the organisation need to contribute to and agree on the route. The result should be something that connects the dots for people in your organisation, showing everyone how their actions fit in with the company's vision. The roadmap should be clear, concise and accessible to all parts of the business.

Once you have your roadmap and have managed to get the energy and resources of the organisation pointing in the same direction, you will need to ensure that you have the capability and capacity to make digital transformation happen. That's where gap analysis comes in, identifying the holes between the capabilities that are available against those that are required to deliver.

Without a realistic plan for digital implementation, an organisation can end up making unfocused digital investments that fail to deliver a return on investment or have any measurable impact on the business goals.

Here are a few things to consider when putting together a roadmap:

1   Start with lighthouse projects

Some digital projects will deliver value quickly while others will take longer. It makes sense for SMEs to start with those that can pay for themselves or at least provide a high enough return to finance the next round of digitalisation. Quick wins also help to build buy-in and momentum.

2   Avoid rigid plans

The digital roadmap should be a regularly reviewed, live document that can flex according to business needs, acting as a consistent reference point to keep everything on track and aligned.

3 Collaborate with all the relevant stakeholders

Although they can only have one overall owner, digital roadmaps should be created and maintained as part of collaborative workshops that involve all relevant stakeholders. This will help to keep initiatives integrated and in line with agreed shared goals.

4 Dependencies

Articulate how everyone and everything is connected, including technology, people, skills, and project management.

5 Value

Include a short assessment of each digital initiative's value against complexity, cost and risk.

Need-to-know workout tips: six reasons why you need a roadmap

1 Gives focus and direction and enables the shift from planning to execution.
2 Encourages collaboration and builds consensus on the best route to your destination.
3 Identifies and co-ordinates the interdependencies of steps along the route.
4 Improves communication by providing a living, visual representation of strategic goals, timelines and intermediate stops on your journey to digital fitness.
5 Helps to plan human resource requirements and operational needs.
6 Helps to prioritise and plan budgetary requirements.

Step 6: Tracking progress

It takes commitment to start the digital fitness programme. It takes determination, stamina and resilience to see it through. There will be times when it's tempting to throw in the towel. I like Rosabeth Moss Kanter's observation that "everything can look like a failure in the middle", that tricky point during the implementation of change when even true believers develop some doubts. That can happen when revenue isn't growing fast enough. Perhaps employees are becoming change weary and naysayers are becoming louder. The temptation to quit looms large.

As she rightly says, "everyone loves inspiring beginnings and happy endings; it is just the middles that involve hard work". Those who master change, persist and persevere. They expect to encounter obstacles on the road to success and celebrate each milestone. They keep arguing for what matters. To keep everyone else on side, leaders must ensure that their get fit for digital roadmap includes key performance indicators to measure progress against goals.

Those goals are the little wins that together propel us towards bigger successes and ultimately lead to the realisation of our vision. The overall vision and transformation goals are inextricably linked. Each provides motivation for the other. That's why many millions of people all over the world have enthusiastically embraced fitness trackers and apps that help us to set our goals and measure our progression against them.

Thoughtful business objective setting (aka targets) is vital because it makes our ambitions more manageable and tangible, spurring us into action with purpose. That's a big driver of motivation which in turn results in higher productivity, less waste, rising revenue, happier employees and satisfied leaders. This is one of the many reasons why an iterative, agile approach to getting digital stuff done is better than more traditional "waterfall" project management methodologies. Lots of incremental gains are simply more motivating than lengthy "Big Bang" projects that may end with a whimper.

Therefore, the first step should be setting those objectives for the implementation plan over a defined period. Setting clear targets at the outset helps maintain momentum and prevents back-sliding when the going gets tough. It also aids the process of prioritising initiatives that will provide maximum impact. Ensure that you set targets for each source of value creation, such as cost savings, revenues, improved performance and satisfaction of employees and customers, as well as new ways of working and the development of new capabilities. But don't get too carried away. A memorable few will work better than a forgettable mass.

When you know your targets, you can then set your KPIs to track the progress against those objectives.

[A Key Performance Indicator: a measurable value that demonstrates how effectively a company is achieving its key business objectives. Organisations use KPIs to evaluate their success in reaching targets.]

A good example of a KPI is the Net Promoter Score (NPS). This is rapidly becoming an oldie, but it's still very much a goodie. If you don't know it, an NPS details customer attitudes and loyalty by classifying your customers into the following three categories:

- Promoters: customers who would recommend your organisation, product or service to their peers (ranks 9–10).
- Passives: customers who like your company yet wouldn't actively recommend it (ranks 7–8).
- Detractors: customers who would actively not recommend your organisation, product or service (0–6).

Subtracting the detractors from the promoters reveals your NPS. This KPI helps to demonstrate how closely your new initiative is aligned to customer needs and provides a reading of your progress against your target – to reach an average NPS of 9 within two years, say.

The other KPI banker is of course ROI. It can be applied in lots of different ways, but the bottom line is always the same: what return did we get on our investment? Just because you need to shift your thinking to focus on the customer, doesn't mean that you don't need to check that it's paying off financially.

Need to know workout tips: six ways to maintain momentum

1 Tune into the environment: what has changed since you began the initiative? Do the original assumptions hold? Is the need still there?
2 Check the vision: does the idea still feel inspiring? Is it big enough to make extra efforts worthwhile?
3 Test support: are supporters still enthusiastic about the mission? Will new partners join the initiative?
4 Examine progress: have promises been kept and milestones passed? Are there early indicators, tangible demonstrations, that this could succeed? Can the next wave of results sustain supporters and silence critics?

5   Search for synergies: can the project work well with other activities? Can it be enhanced by alliances?
6   Identify and deliver quick wins: keep momentum going by demonstrating benefits from quick wins while longer projects are in progress.

Bibliography

Abramovich, Giselle (2012) P&G's New Approach to Digital (March). Available at https://digiday.com/marketing/pgs-new-approach-to-digital/ (accessed 14 April 2018).

Brainyquote.com (n.d.) BrainyQuote. Available at www.brainyquote.com/quotes/nathaniel_branden_163773 (accessed 22 March 2018).

Davidi, Adam (2014) Building Communities with Lego: Let the Users Do the Heavy Lifting (16 April). Available at www.theguardian.com/media-network/media-network-blog/2014/apr/16/lego-building-communities-fans-brands (accessed 4 December 2017).

Farfan, Barbara (2018) Mission Statements of Technology Companies (29 August). Available at www.thebalancesmb.com/tech-companies-mission-statements-4068549 (accessed 10 December 2017).

Hyken, Shep (2016) How Effective Is Net Promoter Score (NPS)? (3 December). Available at www.forbes.com/sites/shephyken/2016/12/03/how-effective-is-net-promoter-score-nps/#4489a0df23e4 (accessed 10 November 2017).

Kanter, Rosabeth Moss (2009) Change Is Hardest in the Middle Available at https://hbr.org/2009/08/change-is-hardest-in-the-middle (accessed 12 February 2018).

McKinsey Quarterly (2018) Data as Jet Fuel: An Interview with Boeing's CIO (January). Available at www.mckinsey.com/business-functions/mckinsey-analytics/our-insights/data-as-jet-fuel-an-interview-with-boeings-cio (accessed 14 November 2017).

Milnes, Hilary (2015) How Burberry Became the Top Digital Luxury Brand (December). Available at https://digiday.com/marketing/burberry-became-top-digital-luxury-brand/ (accessed 12 December 2017).

Available at https://en.wikipedia.org/wiki/Operating_model (accessed 11 March 2018).

SMART Objectives (n.d.) Available at https://en.wikipedia.org/wiki/SMART_criteria (accessed 13 March 2018).

Part 3

The programme

The six components of digital fitness

That's the process. Now let's look at the six components (shown in Figure 2) that every leader needs to focus on in order to get their organisation fit for digital business. These are Mindset, Core strength, Skills, Power, Data and Agility. Within each component there is a "six pack" of workouts. These are the focus areas that together will get an organisation in great shape for a digital future.

Figure 2 Get fit for digital business components

Component 1: Mindset

Figure 3 Mindset six-pack

Commit to fit

All of us have the right to remain fat or skinny or weak. But we know that every workout we miss can make our belly bigger, our muscles weaker and possibly our lives shorter. We are only human and real life often gets in the way. It's the same in business. There's a big difference between simply signing up for change and getting it done.

The fact is that change doesn't come easily. We get emotionally attached to the old ways of doing things. Change takes us all out of our comfort zones, making us prone to procrastination. In my experience, digital business improvement projects can be at best delayed, and at worst derailed, without the commitment and buy-in of all the members of a leadership team. For that reason, it's not enough to commit yourself. You have to persuade the rest of the leadership team to commit with you.

Often, it's your fellow business leaders who need convincing. There are a number of techniques that I have used successfully, particularly when working with leaders who are less keen to engage with change. These are:

1   The demonstration

This involves graphically exposing customer pain points. One way of doing this at low cost is to undertake user testing, deploying an on-demand, online service to show how users struggle with your website or app. (You can find providers for this service by putting "user testing" into your favourite search engine). The company we used would source members of the public, who fitted our customer profile, and ask them to perform specified tasks such as making a purchase, on the website we were assessing.

As part of the service we would get a video showing the tester's PC, phone or tablet screen, so that we could see how the users were interacting with the website or app. Crucially, we could hear the testers too. We would then edit the video footage, stitching the highlights of various testers together with captions emphasising any customer pain points.

This was a powerful tool in persuading leaders of a need for change, as they saw how the testers were struggling and verbally expressing their frustrations. Phrases like "I would never use this company again" were commonly heard, as were a number of other words that I won't repeat here. It became a very powerful way of connecting leaders to their customers; it's one thing to be told there are issues with a website, it's another thing to see and hear it in graphic tones from the people who ultimately pay the wages.

2   Lighthouse projects

These are pilot projects intended to provide a catalyst for change. They are effectively show cases that aim, besides their original purpose, to have a signal effect for numerous follow-up projects, acting as a case study and hopefully as inspiration and guidance.

3   The data

Connecting business leaders to the data is another powerful way of initiating change. In practice this means agreeing the critical few KPIs that they want to see and ensuring that the review of these KPIs is the first point on the agenda in business trading review meetings. The data will draw people in and generate questions. If the answers are available, the value of the data becomes apparent. If it isn't, it should signal the need to improve data capture and analysis capability. The more data becomes used as a basis for discussion, the more habitual its usage becomes.

4   Customer journey workshops

The importance of the customer journey analysis really can't be overestimated as a digital business driver. First and foremost, it directs everybody's attention to the customer and their frequently convoluted journey to purchase. This exercise also reveals customer pain points and opportunities to add value. It uncovers how your team can and must collaborate more effectively to fix those issues and take advantage of those opportunities. Customer journey workshops are a great way to get people from different functions together to focus on the customer. By co-operating in an effort to improve customer experience, a deeper understanding of the need to work together across functional areas is developed. I cover this in more detail in the "Core strength" section.

Disrupt yourself

As a leader, you may need to begin by disrupting yourself. We all need to start thinking differently if we want to do things differently. In order to shift an organisation from simply *doing* digital to *being* digital, leaders need to embrace three ideas. First, they need to have a "growth mindset". Second, they need to develop a "leadership philosophy" that is appropriate for the digital business age; and third, they should adopt the principles of Design Thinking. Let's take a look at each of these in turn.

The concept of a growth mindset was developed by psychologist Carol Dweck and popularised in her book, *Mindset: The New Psychology of Success*. She characterises a growth mindset as an appetite for personal development and an openness to new ideas and opportunities. Traditionally, desirable leadership qualities have included strength, decisiveness and the ability to successfully implement a plan.

Today, in the digital age, such traits remain important, but must now be blended with other skills such as co-operation, collaboration, curiosity and adaptability. Leaders need to be willing to learn and open to change, always looking for new ways of improving customer experience and unleashing the full potential of their team members. They must be able to free their thinking from the strictures of the past. Then, crucially, they must instil that growth mindset in everyone within their team, thus empowering them to think differently.

Top sports coaches talk about their leadership philosophy, the personal code they use to guide their decisions and behaviours on a daily basis. It's common practice in the armed services too; in the United States, the leadership programme at the Army War College in Pennsylvania includes an advanced course actually entitled "The Philosophy of Leadership". However, it's more unusual to hear about personal leadership philosophies in the world of commerce, particularly within SMEs.

Fundamentally, a leadership philosophy is about attitude and values, a collection of ideas that encapsulate everything a business leader does. It articulates what is expected from employees and what they can expect from their leaders. A clear leadership philosophy will influence the way in which you exercise control, select and manage employees and maintain operational quality.

It helps to establish the ground rules and core values, helping leaders to build relationships with their team by bringing consistency and clarity to the workplace. It becomes the embodiment of how you are perceived, your management style and the way in which you handle each situation you face.

It's worth taking a bit of time to step back and reflect on your own leadership philosophy. Digital should prompt a questioning and rethinking of assumed certainties. It may inspire a change in the attitudes and behaviours that are getting in the way of effective leadership in a changed business world. It should reflect the need to listen more closely to customers, institutionalise learning and encourage closer collaboration and continuous improvement on behalf of those customers.

[Design Thinking: an approach towards problem-solving that puts end users and customers at the centre of the design process. The goal is to develop useful products and solutions that fit the needs of the user, not the other way round.]

Leaders can also encourage Design Thinking to embed a customer-centric mindset within an organisation and help even the most traditional thinkers to develop new, more imaginative ways of creating value. Put simply, Design Thinking is a process that helps us to better understand our users and customers. It helps us to challenge assumptions and identify alternative ways of doing things. Think of it as a "working backwards" method, whereby you start with those customer needs and then work out how you can meet them.

Above all, it's a hands-on, people-focused methodology that allows us to spend less time planning and more time doing. There are several variants of the Design Thinking process in use today and you can see the five stages, based on those proposed by the Hasso-Plattner Institute of Design at Stanford (aka "d.school"), in Figure 4. It isn't necessarily a step-by-step process; the stages don't have to follow any specific order and can often occur in parallel to one another.

Leaders in most organisations don't need to be digital business specialists; it's not their job to be experts in all the digital minutiae. But they do need to focus on adapting their leadership style to suit the new business environment. That comes from an understanding of digital operating models and knowing how to bring out the best in people working in a digital business ecosystem. It may mean moving out of comfort zones, as well as challenging habitual mindsets and any assumptions made about what it means to lead a more digital business.

Today, when there are so many moving parts, it becomes impossible for leaders to maintain complete control over day-to-day operations. Making every decision themselves just slows things down. They need to adapt to a new management style whereby they delegate more and trust their people to deliver. That leap of trust is essential. By handing accountability and autonomy to the team, one avoids the parent/child relationships that can be pervasive within SMEs.

Currently, many businesses are still led by digital immigrants but increasingly we see that many of the workforce are digital natives. This can cause fault lines and rifts between leaders and followers if they fail to find a common language. Leadership has always required a rare mix of soft skills. In the digital age those skills are more important than ever. Leaders of modern organisations must be open to new ideas and constructive challenges as well as encouraging the ownership of ideas and projects.

Today, corporate dictatorship is unlikely to get the best out of employees, but that doesn't mean that leaders should let go of the reins. Strong leaders provide a solid strategic framework within which their people work, thus freeing them to get on with that work. They set clear objectives, measured by carefully defined KPIs, and manage the organisation's resources effectively, from team formation to budget allocation. The best leaders tend to intervene only to coach, to remove barriers or to clarify the priorities, focusing their energies on providing direction, motivation and clear performance standards.

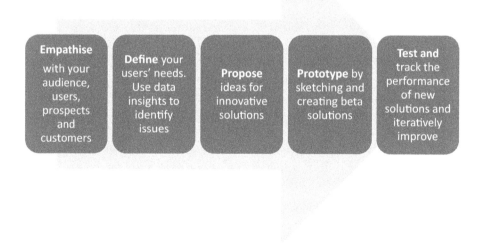

Figure 4 A design thinking process

When you boil it right down great leadership is really about getting a diverse group of people working together reasonably harmoniously, pulling together with a common focus and cause. I say *reasonably* because a bit of "creative tension" is always required. If that's absent, it could be that people are not contributing wholeheartedly or are suppressing their views in order to keep the peace.

Some conflict is an inevitable part of working on a team and, while it's sometimes uncomfortable, it can also be healthy, particularly if the team members are bound together by a common purpose, values and identity. Leaders must communicate through both hearts and minds to lead through change and must develop an *espirit de corps*. They must encourage in their team a commitment to the mission and each other, with a togetherness that feeds off success and pulls them together in failure.

Above all, remember the words of Peter M. Senge: "People don't resist change. They resist being changed".

Get in the zone

It's not just athletes who need to "get in the zone" in order to maximise their performance. Leaders must help to create a kind of team "flow" to achieve digital fitness in their team. Flow develops when people are fully immersed and feel positive about the goal. Earlier I talked about the power of a vision to inspire and drive your journey to digital fitness and the need to warm up your team for change. Now let's look at how you can practically create the conditions for flow to emerge, ensuring that everybody is fully focused and in the zone.

Having laid down the challenge, leaders must communicate the process and components of the change programme. Having a workout plan ready to put into action reassures team members and reduces decision fatigue, leaving them with more willpower and mental capacity to focus on making that plan a reality.

Next, leaders must seek to create an open environment to ensure that any problems in the programme are identified and brought to light. This can be challenging, as people tend to be careful about what they say around people in positions of authority. In many SME cultures it's not done to disagree with the boss in public or to challenge a colleague's pet project. But good leaders want people at all levels to be straight with them, particularly those who are close to customers on a daily basis.

Everyone needs to feel that they have permission to be honest and frank. Regular review meetings can help by allowing employees to share ideas and feel that they are being heard. These feedback sessions can help leaders to get ahead of employee issues before they become a major roadblock to the success of the programme. Such forums, where participants can be free of distractions, help leaders and their teams to begin to collaborate in new ways, working together on overcoming shared challenges, while also identifying shared opportunities for success.

But it's worth bearing in mind that not everyone will feel free or comfortable enough to discuss issues publicly. They may worry about saying something unpopular or feel that they have been put on the spot. Wise leaders will therefore initiate more one-on-one, casual conversations, so that their people are given other opportunities to express their views. Another technique is to take frequent short and snappy surveys that "take the pulse" during the programme.

A leader also needs to take a proactive approach to the politics and emotions that are churned up by change. One effective method is to identify the major influencers within each function or group in the business. Influencers are those who have the resources, skills and networks needed to win over the hearts and minds of the wider group.

It's important to spend time up front identifying these key influencers, listening to their ideas and encouraging their participation. Not only because they are likely to understand the issues at the sharp end, but also because they have the ability to shine either a positive or negative light on proposed changes. Take them out to lunch individually and ask for their feedback. It's important to establish where they stand as the programme progresses. Ellen R. Auster and her co-authors suggest assessing the various influencers' receptiveness to change into the following six categories in their book *Strategic Organizational Change*:

- Sponsors;
- Promoters;
- Indifferent fence-sitters;
- Cautious fence-sitters;
- Positive sceptics;
- Negative sceptics.

When you have identified them, you can then bring sponsors and promoters on board during the initial phases of change. Their energy can greatly assist attempts to win over a fence-sitting majority. Positive sceptics can be useful too, helping to constructively critique various aspects of a plan. Negative sceptics and their concerns will need to be addressed and greater involvement in the planning process may help to calm the fears lying behind their objections. Engaging sceptics can be a strong signal that transparency and openness really are valued and not just paid lip service.

1   Provide background information: be inclusive and facilitate the discussion of the market trends, customer demands, competitive pressure, and other key issues that have implications for the future.

2   Involve team members from all functions early in the process: it will, of course, take longer, but when people are asked for their input and are involved in decision-making early in the game, they are more likely to buy in during and after implementation of change.

3   Agree the fundamental principles: these are the non-negotiable pillars of your get fit programme. Defining and agreeing these collaboratively will help to mitigate internal politics because it nudges people towards decisions based on shared agreements over personal preferences. "Customer first" is a typical pillar.

To get buy-in necessitates making a persuasive case for change, using the fitness assessment findings. You need to show how it will benefit both the company as a whole and individuals by making their jobs easier or even more interesting. Emphasise how change can contribute to their personal development as they learn new, relevant skills. Most of all, bear in mind that what individuals really want to know is how change will affect them and their role.

Despite our best efforts as leaders, sometimes there are pockets of resistance that can't be overcome. I have been involved with transformation projects where individuals simply won't respond positively to any suggestions for change and, worse still, actively seek to undermine it. This can be very damaging, not just to change implementation but also to the health of a company's culture.

In such situations, leaders need to be ready to take some tough decisions. Leadership is, of course, not all hearts and flowers. Sometimes you have to prise the barnacles off the boat. New business practices may need some new blood if the incumbents are simply not willing or able to move with the times. As Jack and Suzy Welch point out in their book *Winning*, "fires" can be as important as "hires". It may be "easier to change the people than to change the people" as the old saying goes, but it's important not to throw out the proverbial baby with the bathwater.

Digital may be forcing change in business, but many of the core skills of digital immigrants remain as essential to a company's operations as ever. Being less digitally literate doesn't make somebody suddenly worthless, any more than being a digital native makes someone an expert in doing business digitally.

When leaders wholeheartedly embrace digital it can result in a productive blend of their experience and perspective with the energy and innovation of digital natives. When leaders fail to embrace digital it can produce tensions, as younger employees become frustrated with what they (probably correctly) perceive to be old school ways of working. But sometimes a new vision requires new people to create it. You need to achieve a balance of people with strong commercial, customer and product knowledge (and the flexibility to adapt and modernise) with those with specialist digital business knowledge. This is an equilibrium that many organisations have so far yet to find, both in their teams and their boardrooms.

We can look to Jim Collins and Jerry Porras for some of their customary wisdom: "Building a visionary company requires one percent vision and 99 percent alignment". The point in this context is that without alignment and buy-in from the wider team, leaders cannot expect to get their organisations fit for digital. That buy-in is unlikely to happen spontaneously. Leaders of SMEs must get everyone involved in the specifics of the conversation.

Earlier, I talked about the power of asking "why". That simple word comes into its own again when leaders need to get their teams in the change zone. They can use it to get the conservation going about the need for change. It's an important part of the important loosening-up process, encouraging colleagues to identify and explore the possible outcomes if the organisation changes – or doesn't.

Here are some categorised questions that can frame that discussion:

Customers

- Why do we need a clearer picture of our customers/audience?
- Why do we need to fully understand their digital research and purchase journeys?
- Why do we need to make it easier for customers to buy from us and communicate with us seamlessly using digital channels?
- Why are we using these marketing channels?
- Why do we need a digital value proposition?
- Why do we need to make our marketing more integrated?
- Why do we need to make our stories more engaging and relevant?
- Why do we need to actively help and encourage our customers to become advocates for our products and services?

Competition

- Why is digital a threat to our enterprise?
- Why is it an opportunity?
- Why are customers migrating to competitors?

Organisation and resources

- Why do we need to develop new skills and capabilities?
- Why do we need some extra resources to implement our get fit for digital programme?

- Why are we doing things this way?
- Why are we budgeting in this way?
- Why are we organised and structured this way?
- Why are we measuring things this way?
- Why are we using this technology?

Leadership and strategy

- Why do we need a change programme, strategy and roadmap?
- Why do we need senior management to review, authorise and champion digital innovation?
- Why are people resisting digitisation?
- Why does everybody in the organisation need to be involved and supportive of this change programme?

Often, these questions lead to further questions and start a wider process of review and discovery. They can also be useful in terms of kick-starting greater collaboration between different functional areas.

Resistance training

Despite a leader's efforts to be proactive by creating the conditions for everyone to get in the zone, an organisation's journey to digital fitness will inevitably cause contention. Leaders must be ready to react when confronted by doubters, acting decisively to prevent the contagion of negative sentiments. Staff trapped in a "fixed" mindset can put the brakes on digital business transformation initiatives.

In the "Warming up" section in Part 2, I touched on some of the real reasons why people can be resistant to change. Resistance is often seen as a negative force during transformation projects. However, properly understood and managed, it doesn't need to be a show-stopper and can actually help to improve the transformation project. Over the years I've seen people dragging their feet, attempting kick projects into the long grass, telling everybody who will listen that digital is not relevant to the company or to their bit of the business and that they have more important things to do right now.

I've worked with some who nod enthusiastically in meetings but who then grumble to colleagues around the water dispenser. Some people take a lot of convincing, particularly in long-established businesses where employees have become very set in their ways. That means you may need to invest some time understanding what motivates people to change and why they can resist it.

This part can't be side-stepped if you're serious about making change happen. It's not unusual for each department to act as an independent fiefdom within organisations, designing and managing their respective touchpoints differently and adhering to differing standards and metrics. This can have a hugely negative impact on customer experience in the digital age.

Here are some of the specific resistance issues I've come across when working with individuals in the past:

1 *Uncertainty about the future*: people tend to shy away from change if it feels like they're jumping out of a plane without a parachute. They may think that an unsatisfactory present is preferable than an uncertain future. Leaders need to communicate clearly and often about the planned change in order to create certainty, providing transparent processes, simple steps, roadmaps and timetables.

2 *Perceived loss of power*: digitally driven change disrupts the status quo and can make people feel that they've lost control over their functional areas. Smart leaders will leave space for those affected by change to make choices, where possible inviting them to take part in the planning process and giving them ownership.

3 *Unpleasant surprises*: don't wait to present people with a finished plan that will surprise them. Imposing change on people suddenly, with no time to get used to the idea or prepare for the consequences, is a surefire way to generate resistance. Leaders should avoid the temptation to plan changes in secret and then announce them all at once. They must paint a vivid picture of why change is necessary, having first planted some seeds and sought input.

4 *Too much too soon*: help people to adapt to their new routines incrementally, so that the shock of change is not too uncomfortable. Prioritise the main things to ensure that the workplace world is not turned upside down, all at once.

5 *Losing face*: when you're suggesting change, take care to recognise good work that has been done in the past, so that those who are closely associated with it maintain some dignity throughout the transition. Together with a clear message about how the world has changed, that can really help people to let go of the past, let down their defences and move on to the future.

6 *Competence concerns*: resistance to change often masks deep concerns in people about whether their skills remain relevant and whether they will be able to transfer them into new ways of working. Leaders should work to allay such fears with information, education, training and appropriate support. They should also work with individuals to define the "how" and their individual objectives within the change.

7 *Increasing workload*: there's no getting away from it – change creates more work in the short term. It is likely that people will be overloaded at times, particularly when there are inevitable setbacks in the process of change. Leaders should take time to understand the day-to-day routines of the people involved in the change and provide appropriate support, such as backfilling business as usual tasks with other staff. They should recognise and reward the exceptional efforts that may be necessary, connecting individuals who will work well together and support one another.

8 *Unintended consequences*: change can create ripple effects that are not always anticipated. There may be unexpected disruptions to other functions, customers and partners in the value chain. These are likely to provoke a negative reaction as no one likes to be affected by change that they had no input in creating, particularly when that change interferes with their own activities. Leaders should think about widening the circle of stakeholders, ensuring that all affected parties, however marginal, are considered and consulted so that any disruption can be minimised.

9 *Stored resentments*: change can have the effect of reopening old wounds that can undermine motivation and curtail co-operation. Leaders should consider any steps they can take to heal these wounds before they begin to fester and spread infection across the wider team.

10 *Actual professional harm*: last, but by no means least, is resistance to change because it is going to affect peoples' livelihoods. Change is not always painless. Reskilling and re-engineering organisations can mean that some roles are replaced and jobs are lost. Leaders must be as open as possible about the potential consequences of change. If there are negative consequences for some, leaders must be honest, transparent and fair. They must act decisively to avoid prolonged periods of uncertainty.

Managing change is a big part of a leader's responsibility. Therefore, it's important to have some strategies in hand to deal with various kinds of resistance. Opposition to change can come in many guises, from subtle sabotage to outright refusal. It's important to be ready to deal with each of them when self-defence mechanisms are triggered. Although leaders can't always make people feel comfortable about change, they can work to minimise discomfort. Diagnosing the sources of resistance is the first step towards good outcomes.

Release endorphins

When leaders have their teams primed for change, warmed up, bought into the vision and feeling able to contribute and offer feedback freely, leaders need to consider staff motivation and incentives. We know that when we work out, our body releases chemicals called endorphins. These endorphins interact with the receptors in our brains that reduce pain and boost our mood. In business, particularly when going through the stress of change, it's helpful to remember that brain chemistry has a role to play too. As a leader, managing energy in our team, the chemical we should be most interested in is dopamine.

This chemical is often known as the "feel good" neurotransmitter because, when we achieve or succeed, it flows into the brain's reward pathway and makes us feel better. It improves motivation and concentration, inspiring us to recreate past successes so that we can feel that pleasure again.

Earlier, I talked about the importance of get fit targets. Your vision is your ultimate destination, but to motivate everyone to get there it's necessary to break up the journey into smaller, achievable waystations. Collecting repeated wins can chemically inspire us to achieve more by causing a repeated release of dopamine. Conversely, repeatedly failures from poorly set, unachievable targets will be depressing and prove counterproductive. The trick is getting the balance right between the achievable and the ambitious.

Goals are an incentive in themselves. Early in my career, when I was frontline selling, my colleagues are I were very competitive about our relative daily performance. At the end of each day we'd rush to see where we appeared on the league table that showed our personal contribution to the overall sales target, despite the fact that there was no additional financial incentive for top performers.

But in a period of change, more tangible rewards may be required. At work, people are motivated by factors that directly and positively impact their professional and personal lives. Incentives are typically considered at the individual level, defined as either financial or non-financial, internal or external, formal and informal. But it's also worth thinking about incentives at the organisational level. In a digital world, business success depends upon a team ethos more than ever.

Here are a few pointers:

1   Reward behaviour publicly.
2   Smaller, more frequent rewards, tied to the smaller goals, are better than larger, infrequent incentives.
3   Try unexpected rewards; don't promise but surprise with a big thank you.
4   Hard cash is always important, but money shouldn't be considered the primary way of rewarding staff. It's worth trying to be a bit more creative than that.

Ongoing staff incentives can be relatively straightforward to implement if you only sell through a single channel. It's a bigger challenge to keep everybody in a team motivated in an omnichannel sales environment, when your customers interact with you digitally, in person and by phone. It can be particularly difficult when each separate sales function is siloed, often with separate profit and loss responsibility and sales incentives.

When individual sales units are effectively competing with one another, the customer and the business both suffer. The customer gets a frustratingly disjointed experience as they move between channels, and tensions within the business undermine a cohesive team performance.

Many multichannel businesses are currently wrestling with the thorny question of how to incentivise staff for sales that cannot be attributed to a single channel. Today, that can be the majority of sales. It is particularly challenging for those who have traditionally paid commission to their sales people. To reward staff based on the last touch, the actual point of purchase, can ignore the contribution of other staff across the entire customer journey. That is likely to negatively affect morale and motivation.

It's a bit like giving the scorer of a goal or a touchdown all the credit for a winning team performance. They may have got the ball over the line, but they didn't do it on their own. Business, particularly digital business, is a team game. Some functions are goal scorers but others play an invaluable assisting role, helping to get a prospect to the point where they are ready to commit to a purchase.

The answer is either a sophisticated attribution commission structure, where the contribution of everyone is recognised, in percentage terms, for the part they have played in creating each sale. But that is not practical for most SMEs. Instead, consider shifting to reward staff on the basis of whole team performance, based on measures such as sales and customer satisfaction such as NPS. It's much easier to manage and sends a very clear signal to the team about the company's reset priorities.

There's plenty to consider when thinking about how best to get that dopamine flowing. But, in a multichannel sales environment the overriding principles must be to incentivise customer-focused teamwork through improved collaboration, communication and motivation. Those things make the difference between organisations that talk a good game and those that make it happen day after day.

Ultimately, the best way to keep your people motivated and loyal is a healthy culture, whereby an individual's contribution to an effective team effort is recognised and valued. As a rule, organisations run on a culture of fear and sycophancy tend to lose talented people, creating a fundamental barrier to growth. Even more importantly, perhaps, they fail to attract the best new talent, and that's a big problem when deep digital business expertise is in short supply.

Plan to succeed

Getting fit for digital business is a programme to prepare and future-proof your enterprise. It is a series of workout exercises designed to get an enterprise in shape for an increasingly digital world. The good news is that you only have to go through the process once, because it's fundamentally about getting the organisation, in terms of people, processes and platforms, ready to adapt to change itself. It is distinct from your strategy, although it will substantially influence how your strategy develops.

SMEs don't always have a clear strategy. In the course of my consulting and coaching work, I sometimes find a hole where the strategy should be. Sometimes it turns out that there is one, but nobody talks about it. That results in everyone wandering around trying to figure out what's important and what they should focus on in their day-to-day work. Of course, everyone knows the tactics. That's what they are immersed in every day. They know their monthly and quarterly goals. But they don't always know the higher-level strategy from which their goals are supposedly derived. That matters if you want your business to grow.

Why should anyone get excited about their activities at work when they have no idea how fits in with the bigger picture? That strategy must leave room for some iteration, responding to insights gleaned from data and market conditions as you move forward. A rigid five-year strategy just doesn't make sense in the rapidly changing world of digital. So, you need a flexible strategy to clearly describe how you will go about the task of achieving your objectives.

Many of the documents I see in SMEs conflate strategy and tactics. In fact, they can be little more than an embellished laundry list of things they need to do. That's a problem, because if you skip directly from objectives to tactics you end up spending money in the wrong places, prioritising the wrong things and creating an organisation that is confused and disjointed. And that's true of any organisation, of any type, of any size, in any vertical, anywhere in the world.

As a quick recap, in the context of getting fit for digital business: your mission is your "why" (purpose), your vision is *where* you want to get to (the future shape of the enterprise), your objectives are *what* you want to achieve (the tangible outcomes) and your strategy is *how* you will make it happen. Tactics are all the individual activities used to implement the strategy. A good way to think about it is that strategy is about doing the right things, while tactics are about doing them well. Figure 5 provides a brief overview.

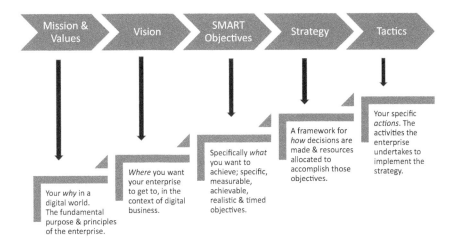

Figure 5 Definitions – from mission to tactics

Component 2: Core strength

Figure 6 Core strength six-pack

Clarity at the core

For humans, core muscles are pretty darn important. They have a major influence on how well your entire body functions and handles everyday activities and tasks. Your posture, breathing, stability, power and flexibility all depend upon a strong core. It's easy to ignore your core until everyday actions become difficult or painful.

As with the human body, a strong business core supports all activities. It is the foundation for digital business success, the main driver of your brand. Most enterprises start with a clear idea of why they are in business and who and what they are for. But as time goes on it's likely that that clarity gets dulled and you risk becoming blind to the reality that other people see. That's particularly true in times of changing customer behaviour, like now. When an enterprise begins to struggle with digital, the root cause often lies within its core.

In our digital fitness programme, the strength of an organisation's core is represented by the clarity of its mission, the degree to which it works to understand its audiences, and the extent to which it endeavours to create ever more value for its customers. Surprisingly, few organisations regularly review their core in response to changes in the market they operate in. This needs to be addressed, as a lack of clarity becomes amplified through digital channels.

Fuzziness at the core, such as having a limited understanding of people's new buying journeys in a connected world, will be reflected in your digital communications, negatively affecting your ability to connect with the right audiences in the right way, using the right channels, at the right time. Equally, it's important to have a well-developed sense of self; namely, who you are as an organisation (your values) and your purpose (your mission).

Every organisation has customers, of course, whether they call them clients, members, guests or passengers. As Peter Ducker memorably observed, the fundamental purpose of business is to acquire and retain those customers. They will also have digital "users", who, although they are not yet customers, are likely to be sales prospects. Being very focused on the needs of users and customers would seem obvious. But as enterprises mature, that focus can become blurred by a growing tendency to see the internal "business" as the primary customer.

Getting fit for digital should prompt a renewed focus on the real customers. We need to know what they look like and, digitally, where they are. We need to be customer-centric in everything we do and that requires the consistent delivery of high-quality and relevant customer experiences that are: (a) co-ordinated to be consistent and joined-up across each channel you use; (b) backed up by ongoing efforts to forge deeper relationships over time; and (c) designed to create a feedback loop with your customers that drives continual improvement and innovation in products, services and overall customer experience.

Just as there are exercises and techniques you can use to improve your physical core, there are ways of building the core strength of your enterprise. In the "Mindset" component, I talked about Design Thinking as a tool that equips teams with a deeper understanding of their customers, so that they can find ways to serve them better. Think of it as Pilates for your business, a practical way to develop a genuine culture of customer centricity.

There are two practical applications of Design Thinking in the context of getting fit for digital business. The first is the act of creating customer personas to help everyone get a more intimate understanding of target audiences. The second is customer journey mapping which can be used to better understand consumers' experience of interacting and buying from you. These two techniques are powerful ways of rallying your team, helping them ask *who* and *why*, so that they can then figure out *how* and *what*.

Know your audience

Start by defining your audience personas. These are based on your audience segments. You have probably identified several of these segments, so create a persona for each one. These pen portraits should provide an instant and human insight into these segments, revealing their attitudes, preferences, behaviours, goals and motivations as they interact with your enterprise. They are an invaluable tool in product design, service packaging and content creation. If you have already created personas, consider revisiting them to see if they remain credible if the context of evolving digital consumer behaviour.

Don't get too carried away by creating too many personas. The idea of having personas is that so that everybody in the business, from the CEO to frontline personnel, can quickly and easily relate ideas to your typical customers. Having lots of personas creates more confusion than clarity, so keep it simple by restricting them to less than six.

It's important to understand that a persona is not based on any specific person, but instead is an abstract representation of many people with similar characteristics. This gets us away from the impossible task of designing our products, marketing and customer service for hundreds or thousands of people in our target audience. It allows us to maintain a high-level understanding of people without having to keep *every* person in mind.

Clearly, these representations must be reliable and realistic, so they are only as good as the (up-to-date) research that sits behind them. It's important that they are based on solid qualitative and quantitative research and web analytics. Use your customer data to build up a picture of your ideal client, and your analytics to see how they are interacting with you online. You can also use social media monitoring software to keep up with what your customers and prospects are saying about you; for example, their positive or negative perceptions and any difficulties they experience when interacting with your business.

By putting a "real" face on your audience segments, it becomes easier to focus and stick with a customer acquisition strategy that meets their particular needs. Over time you can add layers of segmentation and personalisation to further improve your targeting. That will allow you to develop more relevant communications and offers to generate improved conversion rates. Data-rich social media platforms such as Facebook are enabling marketeers to dramatically improve targeting with much deeper levels of segmentation. Almost everything you know about your ideal target audience can be utilised, down to an almost individual level.

As is becoming clearer every year, Facebook knows a great deal about us. It has an intimate knowledge of our interests, not only from our activity on its platform, but also from tracking much of our online activity. A tool called the Facebook pixel allows it to track many of the sites we visit and the purchases we make.

For marketeers, this is targeting gold, giving them the power to go far beyond basic demographic data such as location, gender and age. Facebook's advertising platform allows businesses to create "Custom Audiences" by precisely matching their own customer databases to Facebook profiles using phone numbers, email addresses, Facebook IDs and app user IDs. To expand your reach, you can use their "Lookalike Audiences" option, which does what it says on the tin.

It will become clear when the personas have been adopted by your team when they get on first name terms with them – "Jane wouldn't respond well to that" – and others on the team don't ask who the hell Jane is.

Personas will also help you refine your audience knowledge and move beyond blunt demographics. Demographics can be very misleading on their own. Just think of the often-cited example of Prince Charles and Ozzy Osbourne. They were both born in 1948, grew up in the UK, married twice, have two children, are wealthy and like dogs. Based on their demographic profile they appear similar but it's unlikely they will respond in a similar way to the same marketing message.

Understanding your target audience as real people is a vital step in the development of appropriate value propositions, content, tone of voice and messaging. Those elements are key to establishing the emotional connection that drives a sales pipeline that keeps on giving. As Patricia Fripp succinctly put it, "you don't close a sale, you open a relationship". Developing a deeper relationship with customers should not be solely based on research, whereby customers tell you what they *might* do in the future, but instead it should be based on hard data about who they are and what they *actually do* when they interact with you digitally.

That means building up a picture of customers over time, taking every opportunity to increase your knowledge, so that your marketing and customer experience can continuously evolve to meet their specific needs. I still see organisations, who apparently don't have the budget to invest in digital, continue to spend large sums of money on old school methods of research. It's tough for people in a focus group to answer hypothetical questions, particularly when they relate to products and services of which they have no experience.

The other problem with asking people what they want and what they'd do in any hypothetical situation, is that we are all prone to the odd untruth. Or, to be blunt, we are all liars. Seth Stephens-Davidowitz describes this brilliantly in his book *Everybody Lies*, in which he illustrates the power of data science to work out what makes people tick. To paraphrase his work, we lie about how much we drink and how frequently we go to the gym. We lie about how much those new shoes cost and whether we read that report. We call in sick when we're not and say we'll be in touch when we won't. We lie to our friends, our bosses and our children. We lie to parents and doctors. We lie to partners and we lie to ourselves. We also lie on the surveys we complete.

This won't make me popular with market research companies, but I suggest that you consider shifting at least some of your budget from research to analysis. Today the best way to understand people is to track their behaviour online and use that data to respond appropriately. If you use analytics software, you have the potential for insights that can dramatically improve your business. There are many other useful tools that can show you everything from what products and services people are searching for, through to which websites they are visiting to buy them.

There will always be a place for traditional research techniques. But nowadays, much more can now be done, faster and at considerably less cost, to understand our target audience using a variety of digital tools. For example, analysis of the 2012 U.S. elections by New York Times' Nate Silver showed that Google's fully automated online polls outperformed more traditional telephone methods in predicting the outcomes. As he put it, "we're living in a world where Google beats Gallup".

Know how they buy

The second Design Thinking exercise I like to use on the get fit programme is the creation of a customer journey map. This is a graphical representation of all the places (aka touchpoints) where your customers come into contact with your company, be this digitally or in person. The objective of creating a customer journey map is to get a holistic view of the customer's route to purchase, and understand, from their point of view, what it is really like to buy from you.

It tells the story from initial contact, through the process of engagement, conversion and from there, hopefully into a longer-term relationship. Without a map it's very difficult to ensure that we are visible in all the right places with the right propositions to attract prospects – and then convert them into customers who keep them coming back for more, particularly given that the buying process can be a protracted affair.

The length of the customer journey, in terms of number of days and number of interactions, varies widely depending on the type of purchase, of course. Some decisions require substantial research, while others are made very quickly. Typically, and unsurprisingly, more complex and expensive purchases have longer paths to purchase; holidays, for example, about which multiple people in a household will have a say in the decision-making process. However, for the modern shopper nearly all purchases involve some degree of online research, be that for a car or an accountant, a house or a hair-dryer.

Figure 7 shows the plethora of channels that a customer might touch, as they take a linear path from an initial awareness of your offering, through research to purchase and then advocacy – when hopefully they are so delighted with their experience that they are prepared to endorse you.

But, as we all know from personal experience as shoppers, our journey to purchase may not be that straightforward. The customer journey can take many twists and turns; you need to understand it so that you can be in the right place at the right time with the right message and call to action. A nudge here and there can make a huge difference to your conversion rates.

As Google put it:

> The behaviour of individual shoppers now is iterative and nonlinear . . . Shoppers don't always move through a funnel, narrowing choices as they go . . . they can actually widen their choices. The more they learn, the more options they consider . . . The funnel is now more like a neuron, with branches that let shoppers move forward and backward through the process until they're ready to make a decision.

In essence, it's about identifying what the folk at Google call the "moments that matter" for your customers. Organisations that take the trouble to map their customers' journeys can take great strides forward by working backwards to design a joined up customer experience.

In the digital age, organisations have many more marketing options to generate traffic, leads and sales. An SME doesn't have the resources to do everything everywhere, so it needs to find a way to simplify this process, distilling those options down to uncover the right marketing recipe. That's another reason why customer journey mapping is invaluable.

It is undeniable that a customer's buying experience today is an integral part of marketing. The best content, messaging and calls to action, highly targeted though they may be, will fail to convert prospects into customers if your website is too slow, lacks useful functionality, is difficult to use across different screen sizes, or suffers from customer amnesia. Most people use a combination of devices, perhaps a smartphone on the morning and evening commute, a desktop at work and a tablet or laptop at home, probably dual screening as they watch TV (if they still do) at night.

A major benefit of mapping is that it links customer experience directly to operational improvements. It moves the conversation on from the usual tracking of customer satisfaction along functional lines – how satisfied they are with the service they received from the call centre for example – to a more holistic view from the customer's perspective, as they move between channels and devices. Therefore, it's vital to deliver an *integrated* brand experience to attract customers and drive revenue and growth. Otherwise customers may rate most of their individual interactions with your organisation highly, yet judge their overall experience to be poor.

Earlier in the book, when we looked at definitions of "digital", I talked about SMAC, the acronym for Social, Mobile, Analytics and Cloud. Each area is important in its own right, but the best performance comes from understanding how you can make the four operate together. Let's take a couple of practical examples. You could ask your customers to sign in via one of their social media accounts so that, in addition to an email address, you can access data from their social profiles. Or you could provide buttons that help users to share your content, which they upload from their mobiles to their social networks with a single tap.

Many advanced economies already have over 80 per cent smartphone penetration. Mobile devices now account for the majority of internet consumption worldwide. As a result, the amount businesses shell out on mobile advertising already represents more than 50 per cent of the total digital spend in several countries.

The spread of smartphones and other mobile devices has increased interactions between businesses and consumers as people take the opportunity to connect with them anytime, anywhere. They allow people to get on with their real lives, while easily integrating aspects of their digital lives. It is, of course, much easier to fire off a quick email from a mobile device when you're out and about than to remember to do it when you get back to base.

Therefore, when thinking about how your customers research and buy today, mobile cannot be an afterthought. It needs to be integrated into everything you do and should be at the forefront of your marketing and customer experience strategy.

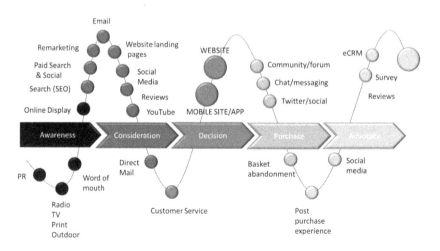

Figure 7 Customer journey mapping

One key moment in the customer journey is the start of the customer's research. This often begins with a search engine. The art and science of staying visible at that crucial initial stage requires constant work and innovation. A good example is the recent rise of voice search, as more and more households start to use Amazon Echo or Google Home devices. The trend for consumers to speak to their digital assistants, rather than to type into search engines, is moving rapidly upwards. That change in consumer behaviour has led innovative enterprises to tailor their SEO strategies so that they become more visible to this growing group of potential customers.

For those who choose customer experience as a key plank of their digital transformation, customer journey mapping is perhaps *the* most important activity you can undertake. Although being customer-centric would seem obvious, in practise it can be tricky to stick to. That's because organisations tend to be made up of specialists, both in-house and in agencies. This mix of specialists can often have the effect of moving the focus away from customers and on to the communication channels or technology.

A good customer journey map can overcome this. It can and should be the key business tool for aligning customer priorities with the behind-the-scenes systems, teams and operations that deliver them. More than that it becomes the catalyst for collaboration across functional areas, the means of identifying the right technology, and a framework for measuring success. It will also help you to prioritise the projects on your roadmap and benchmark your customer experience against competitors. Again, this does not only apply to big organisations. Every business can benefit enormously from this customer clarity.

There are different ways to undertake customer journey mapping (aka customer experience maps), depending on the business type, service or product being considered. But common to them all is the need to look in more detail at each touchpoint within the journey to purchase, testing them against the criteria of your personas and value propositions. Ask yourself:

- Does this match up to the value proposition?
- Does this meet the needs for this persona?

The objective is not only to create a clear understanding of the prospects' interaction with your brand, but also to identify external influencers and other intermediaries that affect their decision-making.

Qualitative insight

- Use a framework of "doing, thinking, feeling" for each touchpoint to record how a persona is reacting.

Quantitative information

• Use surveys and analytics data to measure how many prospects encounter a given touchpoint and track how many of those move on to the next stage of your sales funnel (something we look at later in "Digital selling").

A final suggestion: make your customer experience maps large in scale and actionable in content – and remember that a good customer experience map is the start of a truly customer-centric culture, the beginning of an ongoing process, not a set and forget piece of work.

Need-to-know workout tips: ten ways to drive a more customer-centric culture

1 Undertake a process to create your customer personas from your audience segments.
2 Carry out collaborative workshops to map your customers' journeys.
3 Encourage all your employees to experience the company's products and services in the same way that a customer would online and offline. This is important whether you are B2B or B2C.
4 Encourage your team to share their experiences of the good, the bad and the ugly.
5 Ensure that as a leader you talk directly to customers at least twice a month.
6 Create ongoing customer feedback loops, for example through short online surveys and satisfaction score selections.
7 Study your customer reviews once a month. If you don't have reviews start them; they are major conversion drivers online, assuming that you have a good product and mostly happy customers.
8 Regularly undertake online user testing where the voices and mouse cursors of users are captured on video as they try to complete tasks on your website or app.
9 Go back onto the shop floor, in whatever form that is, throughout the year. Leaders always benefit from regular stints on the front line.
10 Share and shadow: encourage your people to talk to each other and experience life in another function. Cross-functional collaboration is key to driving a customer-centric culture.

Know the market

Business leaders know that when they are launching a start-up, they need to intimately understand the marketplace in which they intend to operate. That's obvious. But I think it's now equally important for leaders of established businesses to formally review the marketplace on a more regular basis, because it's likely, largely due to digital, that a lot of change is happening.

To begin with, market trends may have changed within the industry, and, hand in hand with that, your competitors may not be the ones you have been used to do dealing with. It's not always just a trading issue. It may be that you want to attract investment for the next growth phase of the organisation and you need to demonstrate to potential investors that you have an intimate knowledge of your market, particularly with reference to digital disrupters.

Typically, this analysis will provide a comparison of your competitors' positioning and a description of their strengths and weaknesses in the context of new technology. It should also examine changing customer behaviours and emerging changes in the competitor landscape. A key part of market analysis should be to get into the detail of the drivers of demand for your product or services. You can then benchmark your competitors against each of these, such as customer experience, price, quality, convenience, add-on services, and so on.

Keeping an eye on the competition is always worthwhile, particularly in times of rapid change. Some business commentators advise against competitor analysis, saying that it can distract an organisation from evolving in its own way. I don't agree. I am not proposing that you obsess about them, but it can be very useful to see the sort of things they are doing and spot any developing trends.

Amazon's attitude is that "although leaders pay attention to competitors, they obsess over customers". Amazon has built up its dominant position in the market by understanding that value is created, not only through the features, benefits and price of its products, important as those are, but from the broader customer experience, where easy-to-use customer interfaces, seamless interactions and fast delivery matter just as much.

There are some obvious things to do when monitoring the competition, such as following them on social media, subscribe to their marketing emails and blogs, sign up for their newsletters and set up appropriate Google alerts. Review their content and strategy to see who they have identified as their target audience. Get a good understanding of their positioning. You could research the keywords they are targeting for their search engine marketing, analyse the placement of their digital advertisements and get a good idea of their website traffic volumes and where those visitors are coming from.

There are a range of tools available to help you to do this, or you can get a specialist to do it for you. You should also periodically buy products from competitors, testing scenarios based on getting to different stages on the customer journey to see how they react to keep customers on the hook. You can even run low-cost usability testing on their websites, using online services to see how easy (or not) it is to use your website in comparison to theirs.

This kind of research and analysis will help you to understand their digital sales funnels and the kind of customer experience they provide. The data you can collect on your competitors includes:

- Insights into their overall digital strategy.
- Where they get their website traffic.
- The specific audience segments they target.
- Their market positioning and key campaign themes.
- The digital channels within which they are most active.
- Their content marketing lures; what free information, functionality and resources they offer to encourage users to give their email address.
- The email prospect cycles they run to convert prospects into customers.
- How they encourage reviews and social media advocacy.
- How they reach out to influencers, such as expert reviewers.
- How they keep customers coming back for more.

It also makes sense to revisit the ongoing question of barriers to entry into your market. Investors will certainly want to know what prevents someone from metaphorically opening a shop in front of yours and taking 50 per cent of your business. There can be many barriers, but you need to be realistic. Having a great website is not in itself a convincing barrier to entry. But if the customer experience you provide is exceptional, because of your unique technology for example – well, that is another story.

Here are a few examples of barriers to entry:

- *Investment*: businesses that require a substantial upfront investment.
- *Technology*: sophisticated and ideally unique technology.
- *Brand*: the substantial marketing costs required to get to a certain level of awareness and recognition.
- *Regulation*: licences and concessions in particular.
- *Access to resources*: exclusivity with suppliers, proprietary resources.
- *Access to distribution channels*: exclusivity with distributors, proprietary networks.

Some potential barriers are a little more ambiguous. For example, if you have built great visibility in search engines for relevant and popular keywords, that is an excellent source of business. But leaders and investors have to remain mindful that things can change quickly. For example a single update to a search engine algorithm can have a dramatic effect on the visibility of a brand for popular search terms. Should such a change prove negative, a key source of competitive advantage can almost disappear overnight.

Know your purpose

Having a thorough understanding of the market, particularly in the context of digital, can act as a powerful catalyst for change. But in the end leaders know, like great sports coaches, that as a team they are mainly competing against themselves. It's not about what's happening around us or what's happening to us. Typically it's more about what's happening inside us as businesses. It is a waste of emotional energy to focus too much on things you can't directly control. So, keep most of your focus on the controllable stuff within your own business and remember that the biggest opportunities are often to be found within the organisation itself. Start with your mission.

[A mission: this is a short statement about an organisation's purpose and identifies the scope of its operations: what kind of product or service it provides; its primary customers or markets; and its geographical region of operation.]

Here's an example of how *not* to do it: "It is our mission to continue to authoritatively provide access to diverse services to stay relevant in tomorrow's world."

Feeling inspired? No? This is typical of many mission statements. Boring mumbo jumbo. Uninspiring and unintelligible. You will no doubt be familiar with the idea of mission and value statements. You may well already have them. Or you may think they are a classic example of fluffy things that agencies tout but don't really add much value.

Like a "vision", I think that mission statements are increasingly important in a digital world because they help clarify purpose and build trust. Earlier, I talked about why setting a renewed vision for your organisation is so important to show everyone where you are headed. A mission statement articulates what you will focus on every day in order to reach that destination. It helps to ensure that you don't get lost along the way. If your final mission statement fails to excite you, then the chances are that it hasn't been properly thought through. What does a good mission statement look like? Well, I think eBay does a pretty good job with the following: "Provide a global trading platform where practically anyone can trade practically anything".

Here are a few more:

- Google's aim is "to organize the world's information and make it universally accessible and useful".
- Ben & Jerry's aim is "making the best possible ice cream, in the nicest possible way".
- Charles Schwab's is "helping investors help themselves".
- comScore seek "to leverage the power of the internet to increase the effectiveness and efficiency of our clients' sales and marketing efforts".
- Disney's goal is "to make people happy".

Of course, these are all large companies with a global reach. I have just used them for comparison. SMEs may want to be more specific about their scope, perhaps highlighting products, customer segments and specific market geographies.

By the way, the mission statement quoted at the beginning of this section was created by the online "Mission Statement Generator", which rearranges words into proto-typical mission statements full of meaningless corporate speak. If you had time you could search for it and have a play. But you probably have more important things to do.

[Value proposition: (in marketing) an innovation, service, or feature intended to make a company or product attractive to customers.]

It is, of course, important to effectively communicate your key message, your mission, to your visitors across your digital assets, especially first-time visitors. Surprisingly, relatively few companies do this well. Your value proposition is how you articulate your offer, the solution to your target audience's needs. The idea is to clearly differentiate your value proposition from the unique selling points of your competitors.

This notion was summed up well by Joe Pullizi when he defined it as the "intersection between what a brand wants to communicate, and what the user wants to find, solve or hear".

It's not always easy. Businesses can be so close to their day-to-day activities that they struggle to stand back and objectively identify what makes them unique and valuable to their customers. It's often useful to have an independent perspective to help to identify the essence of what makes your organisation special, or what makes it stand out from the crowd. As well as working to improve the customer experience, you may also need to look at ways in which you can simplify your product and remove any complexities, making it easier for customers to digitally self-serve.

Earlier, I talked about the insurance start-up Lemonade and how it had simplified the claims procedure for customers, allowing them to submit a claim on video from their mobile phones. They also took the decision to take out a major irritant and point of confusion in their product. By removing the unpopular policy excess, or deductibles as they are called in the United States, they attracted many more insurance buyers and boosted customer loyalty.

Need-to-know workout tips: four steps to creating a meaningful mission statement

1   Use simple language: avoid corporate speak at all costs. Utilise short sentences with a basic structure and vocabulary that can be easily understood by anyone.
2   Show your unique value: this is the hook for your prospects and repeat customers. Whatever product or service you are selling, let your customers know why you are the best choice out there, what their custom will help you to achieve, as well as what you can help them achieve.
3   Make it memorable: if your mission statement can be instantly recalled by any member of your team, and they don't roll their eyes or smirk then you've probably got it right. Even better if it becomes a mantra for them – again without having their tongues firmly in their cheeks.
4   Look at the bigger picture: the best company mission statements include the main reason why the business exists and how it is making the world a better place. That sounds a bit pompous and lofty, but why shouldn't your organisation be a force for good, whatever its scale?

Know your values

[Values: important and lasting beliefs or ideals shared by the members of a culture about what is good or bad and desirable or undesirable. Values have a major influence on a person's behaviour and attitude and serve as broad guidelines in all situations.]

Looking over those real examples of mission statements you may detect some evidence of their company values seeping in. Values are now an essential part of how people, in the transparent online market, make decisions about who they trust and how they spend their money. It's less about statements on your website and more about how your organisation actually *is*, what it really stands for and what makes you different. That may not sound very digital. But online channels and platforms provide the means to tell and amplify your story, and those communications must be underpinned by core values and an intent that is shared and applied consistently across a business.

Think about what is relevant to, and will resonate with, your target audience. Set the positive expectation of what it's like to do business with you. That's the reason almost every website has an "About Us" section. Customers want to know who they're dealing with. Since they won't be seeing them face-to-face they want to get a sense of their credentials and what they stand for. They want to get a feel for the authentic human face behind the slick copy. Customer testimonials and reviews are also very important in this context.

Fundamentally, particularly if they are dealing with you for the first time, prospects and customers want to know if they can trust you, not just with their money but emotionally. That's because, all things being equal, we would all prefer to do business with people we actually like, people who share our world view and values. Most of all, we like authenticity. We like people who consistently keep their promises, even when they know no one's looking. It's called integrity.

A value statement describes what the organisation believes in and how it will behave. It provides the foundation stone of organisational culture and acts as a moral compass for the company and its employees. This in turn guides decision-making and establishes standards against which we can measure our actions.

Of course, it's not enough to simply write them down. That's just box-ticking. Business leaders can't just create a new value statement and expect it to become embedded in the thoughts and actions of its staff. They must also walk the values walk, as part of their leadership philosophy. Their team will take their cue from them. To do that they must understand and fully embrace the values and actively use them to guide attitudes, actions and decision-making on a daily basis.

Unlike mission statements, value statements are not for everyone. Developing a values-led organisation can be a slow and involved process that should be attempted only by those who are willing and able to make a long-term commitment to upholding it. There is no point making promises that you are unwilling or unable to keep. But value statements can be very powerful, effectively providing the emotional element of the vision statement and inspiring the organisation through its journey to digital fitness.

[Company culture: this refers to the beliefs and behaviours that determine how a company's employees and management interact and handle outside business transactions. Often, corporate culture is implied, not expressly defined, and develops organically over time from the cumulative traits of the people that the company hires.]

Everything we've covered so far comes together under the umbrella of company culture. Think of it as the personality of your business; a mix of elements, including leadership, work environment, company vision, mission, values, ethics, expectations and goals. Every organisation, consciously or unconsciously, develops its own culture. You can usually tell a lot about a business within five minutes of arriving at its offices, just in the way it feels. You can immediately get a sense of its energy or the absence of it. It's all the product of an organisation's culture.

It's not about a having a "cool" work space. I've been to some funky offices where, once you get under the skin, you see that the organisation is as hierarchical and traditional as a hospital in the 1960s. Culture is less about image and more about developing the right behaviours. I think Frances Frei and Anne Morriss put it well in the *Harvard Business Review* when they said:

Culture guides discretionary behaviour and it picks up where the employee handbook leaves off. Culture tells us how to respond to an unprecedented service request. It tells us whether to risk telling our bosses about our new ideas, and whether to surface or hide problems. Employees make hundreds of decisions on their own every day, and culture is our guide. Culture tells us what to do when the CEO isn't in the room, which is of course most of the time.

Today, in this digitally transparent business world, your organisation's culture can be just as important as your marketing. In fact, it can be even more important, because perceptions of your culture can have a bigger effect on the people that matter the most – your audience, customers and potential employees. A quick visit to an employee review website, such as Glassdoor, will quickly confirm this.

Before digital allowed people to shine a bright light on every organisation, your internal culture was just that: *internal*. But that has changed. David Mattin expressed it thus:

Now, there's no such thing as "internal culture"... Your culture is totally visible. It's a fundamental part of your brand. And it can be your most powerful public-facing asset or liability ... Your brand is your culture, your culture is your brand.

I also like the way he described the effect of digital on culture and brand, with his "glass box" analogy:

In short: a business used to be a black box. Now, it's a glass box. Back when your business was a black box, the brand was whatever you painted on the outside of the box. You had control over that. People came and looked at what you'd painted, and either they liked it or they didn't. Now, thanks to the radical transparency made possible by a connected world, your business is a glass box. People can see all the way inside. And that means that now the brand is everything they see. Every person. Every process. Every value. Everything that happens, ever. There's a single word that sums up what a person sees when they look deep inside your business: they see your culture.

He goes on to argue that nobody expects your culture to be perfect, but what they will be looking for is a positive commitment to improving that culture. So, it makes sense to tell the story of those efforts rather than a less convincing one of an existing cultural nirvana.

David Ogilvy defined a brand as: "The intangible sum of a product's attributes: its name, packaging, and price, its history, its reputation, and the way it's advertised".

Jeff Bezos' definition is as follows: "Your brand is what other people say about you when you're not in the room".

The word "brand" is defined in many ways. Originally, of course, it referred to a visual representation of an entity, for identification purposes; for example, I know that cow belongs to me because it carries my brand. It is still used to talk about an organisation's logo or trademark, and in this context it's very tangible. But here I'm using the wider definition of brand. That is what your prospects and customers *think* of when he or she hears your company's name. It's not as tangible because it exists only in someone's mind. It is an individual's factual and emotional perception of your business.

To form a positive perception of your brand in the minds of your audience takes a combination of what you say and what you actually do. You can, of course, say what you like about the company but if it's not true it won't take long for word to get around. That was true in a world before the web. But now it can happen much faster and the impact can be much greater. The transparency, speed and viral nature of the web has seen to that. It's easy for businesses to lose sight of their core brand message within the throes of daily commercial life. That's an issue because you don't create your brand and move on. Your brand is a living thing. Your audience's perception is the sum of every interaction they have with your organisation.

We may live in an age of almost perfect information for customers and therefore almost perfect competition. But time and again we have seen how the power of emotion can override data and what we might call rational decision-making. As Blaise Pascal perceptibly commented in his work *On the Art of Persuasion*, written in 1658, people almost invariably arrive at their beliefs not on the basis of proof but on the basis of what they find attractive. He was a French mathematician, logician, physicist, theologian and definitely no fool.

So, developing a memorable, positive brand is pretty important. Perhaps the only exceptions are those retailers whose business is based purely on a commodity model. These businesses focus solely on delivering the lowest possible price, something they can't deliver if they are increasing their costs through brand-building marketing. They become experts in search engine marketing and selling through shopping platforms such as Amazon, eBay, Alibaba and Etsy, leveraging the brand of the selling platform rather than their own, in order to convince prospects that it is safe to do business with them. Often, they are essentially a digital marketing service for drop-ship manufacturers and distributers.

Component 3: Skills

Figure 8 Skills six-pack

Marketing and sales skills

Before leaders can properly plan the configuration of their human resources, they first need to identify the skill sets they need to develop in their existing team, or alternatively buy in. In the new business world that's not as easy as it used to be. When I started working, organisational structures, roles and job descriptions were well established and pretty static. If we wanted to recruit someone, we knew exactly how they would fit in within the team. The chances were that the job description was already on file. All we had to do was send it to the recruitment agency and wait for the CVs to roll in.

Today, it can be a little more complicated. When roles and job descriptions change and evolve after decades of consistency, there's always going to be a learning curve. Things are beginning to change now, but there's still a lot of confusion out there about who does what and the role label we put on them. Both leaders and their HR people may need some help with the process of defining needs, roles and relevant KPIs, if they are to avoid expensive hiring mistakes. There is also the added challenge that, as so often, one size does not fit all. The skill sets you need very much depend on the current level of your organisation's digital maturity, your scale and your vision, mission and strategy.

Let's start by looking at the sales and marketing skills that modern SMEs need to possess in order to succeed in a more digital, direct marketing world.

Successful sales people have always been feted by business leaders, and rightly so. Businesses that don't sell effectively don't last long, no matter how good their products or services. That's why in many traditional businesses the best sales people often out-earn their bosses. On the other hand, marketing people can get a bad rap in the boardroom. Some take the view that they just spend money, rather than bringing it in. In the past, perhaps they did have a point.

Traditionally, the marketing department *has* been a cost centre. That's why, if times get tough, the first thing leaders tend to cut is marketing. It's understandable when they can't see the direct correlation between marketing spend and the revenue that can be directly attributed to it.

An old school SME marketing function felt that its job was to build awareness, present the proposition and bring the customers in through the door or on the phone. Outside of direct marketing (usually direct mail), there was little *direct* accountability for what happened after that. It was somebody else's job to turn that awareness, interest and consideration into pounds, euros or dollars. That somebody would have "sales" in their job title.

Well, not anymore, not in the digital marketplace. Marketing shouldn't be a cost centre anymore, particularly for businesses that sell online. It should be a profit centre. Since almost everything can be tracked, it must now be directly accountable for the efficacy and ROI of marketing spend in terms of customer acquisition and retention. In other words, now that highly trackable digital channels have become central to most purchases, marketing people have had to become sales people too, responsible for revenue as well as cost.

Although larger companies increasingly have dedicated "customer experience" job functions, in most SMEs that responsibility falls to the marketing department for digital sales. They have taken responsibility for, and therefore ownership of the entire customer experience, from awareness through to purchase and beyond into advocacy and retention.

Leaders are therefore asking for a whole new set of skills from their marketing people, and not just digital sales skills. Today, we need such personnel to be more akin to general managers, as they add more analytical, technical, change and project management skills to their core skill set. We will examine those skills in a little more detail shortly. But first let's take a look at what modern marketing entails.

Marketing used to be about attracting customers through paid media (aka advertising), as well as "earned" media (aka public relations, or PR) and good old-fashioned word of mouth recommendations. *Owned* media was usually limited to your brochure or catalogue. Today, we still have *paid* media, although digital has given us many more choices about where to spend our advertising budget. We still have *earned* media too, but now traditional PR has been joined by social media and other user-generated content such as reviews and influencers such as bloggers. *Owned* media has evolved into websites, apps, online communities and our own blogs. So, the marketing media choices now look like Figure 9.

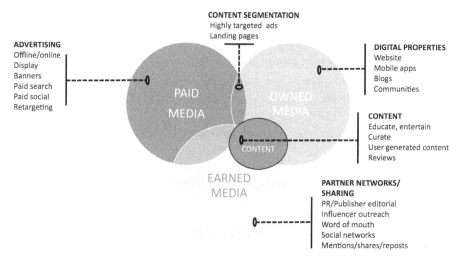

Figure 9   Paid, Owned and Earned Media (POEM)

It's important to understand how these three media categories can work together to achieve results that are greater than the sum of their parts. As digital businesses have matured, the proportion of their marketing budget spent on earned and owned media has tended to overtake that allocated to paid advertising. To understand why paid advertising has become relatively less important, it helps to understand the basic mechanics of modern marketing.

You're busy, so let's boil this down into three main areas and look at the way each works, the contribution they can make to your bottom line, and the implications for the skills that a digitally fit business needs to acquire.

- *Inbound marketing* (aka content marketing): the process of always-on, "pull" marketing to attract qualified prospects to your website.
- *Outbound marketing*: periodic push marketing. Advertising campaigns to build awareness of your product and brand.
- *Customer relationship management* (CRM): nurturing leads and customers to increase conversion, cross-sell and upsell, grow repeat purchasing and encourage advocacy.

Let's look at each of these in a little more detail.

Inbound versus outbound marketing

Would you rather be a marketing pusher or a puller? Most people prefer to be pullers. Nobody really likes pushy. Few of us enjoy cold calling and for good reason. The vast majority of people you call really don't want to speak to you. They are not interested in your offer, or at least they are not interested in talking about it at the time you contact them. Most old school advertising is cold calling of one sort or another. It may not be as intrusive as an unsolicited phone call, but it tends to interrupt us all the same. Traditional advertising is based on a precept of taking our attention away from the article we are reading or the programme we are watching.

None of us like being interrupted, particularly when we have no current interest in the things being pitched to us. There is, of course, an important role for some "push" advertising. It works as part of an overall marketing strategy – otherwise nobody would do it. If you have sufficient budget available, it generates brand awareness and that increases conversion rates from your pull marketing. Today, the best game in town for most organisations, particularly SMEs without powerful brands, is pull marketing, a simple idea that has made Google a digital business superpower.

When search engines came along, everything changed. There was suddenly an opportunity for consumers to look for what they wanted, when they wanted it. More than that, they were given the opportunity to quickly compare quality and price. Suddenly, the scales had shifted to the customer, giving them much better visibility of all the offers out there for a particular product or service. Not only could they immediately research alternatives quickly and easily, but they could also consult the collective experience of other buyers to gauge whether the product lived up to the sellers' promises.

So, search engines and websites were great for buyers. But they were also pretty great for sellers too. Sure, there was more competition. But at least you knew that the people who found their way to your website were likely to be people interested in your offer, assuming you'd worked to ensure it was visible for the relevant keywords.

That was a massive pivot point in marketing; something that we've all begun to take for granted. It meant that anyone, anywhere, could, relatively inexpensively, put their commercial offer in front of well-qualified prospects, rather than people who might fall into a broad group of the *potentially* interested. Hot prospects versus suspects, if you like.

Together with selling platforms like eBay, Amazon and Etsy, it ignited a new economy of small and micro-businesses, collectively challenging the might of the big players by cherry-picking commercial niches on the World Wide Web. Inbound marketing, aka content marketing, is the biggest change in marketing for decades, the product of content plus search engines.

Assuming you have a product or service for which there is a demand, you can pull people to you by creating appropriate content and working to increase links from other websites. Those links, particularly if they are from high-quality websites – as judged by the search engine algorithms – are effectively votes for your website that will improve your website visibility.

Although most businesses have seasonal purchasing peaks and troughs throughout the year, the inbound marketing model recognises that there will be demand throughout the year. That provides a constant opportunity to engage suspects, turn them into qualified prospects, and lead them through your "sales funnel" (more on that shortly).

The bottom line is that nobody wants to chase customers. Why would you go looking for customers, hoping to find people for which the product, price and, critically, the timing of your offer is spot on, when you can pull them to you when they are ready to buy – or at least engage with you. It's really just common sense.

Many start-ups have used Google and the inbound marketing model to establish themselves and acquire customers at low cost through their search engine optimisation efforts. But the smartest have also worked to develop their brand once they have matured as a business. Leaders of those companies understood that merely relying on the ever-changing algorithms of Google for long-term business success is a fool's game. Search engine optimisation, targeting relevant industry keywords, should always be an important part of the marketing mix. But there are significant risks with putting all your eggs into the search engine basket.

The ideal is that people come to your website because they are aware of your brand and already trust you. You want them to immediately think of your business when they have a relevant need, so that they will enter your company name into the search engine rather than generic keywords related to product or service they are after. Therefore, developing a strong, trusted brand can become the best defence against the growing competition and rising costs of being top of the results in search engines.

SMEs may not have the resources to be a brand that it instantly recalled by every consumer everywhere, but they can target their digital and offline advertising, their "paid media", within a limited area – either geographically or within a niche – to build awareness in smaller locations. They can also optimise their "owned media", typically their website, to be more visible within a search engine's local search results. Local SEO is focused on providing results that are relevant to a searcher based on their current location. If I search for 'best bike shop' on my mobile phone or PC right now, Google would prioritise results for the businesses that are physically nearest to me. Focusing on local search can help smaller businesses to become bigger fish in a smaller pond.

Today, it is much harder to get "free" marketing through search engines. The cost of effective search engine optimisation has gone up because you are now competing with more small businesses and most of the big guns. Search engine optimisation has become a marketing arms race as businesses compete on content, links and technical website tweaks to make their business stand out.

This trend has been exacerbated by search engines promoting paid ads and other mechanisms that clutter the search results page and push down the visibility of other "natural" (aka "organic") results. But the pull model is too good to ignore just because it's become harder. You just have to work the "long tail" harder and learn to tell your stories in a more compelling and engaging way.

[Long tail SEO: a technique involving targeting highly specific niche search terms – long tail keywords – that usually consist of three or more words and are easier to rank highly for due to lower competition.]

Whether you are a blue-chip company, a firm of lawyers in Atlanta, or a bike shop in Brighton, you need to demonstrate your expertise digitally by publishing great content. That will always attract links from other websites. In turn, this will help to spread awareness of your brand, reinforcing Google's positive perception of your organisation and helping you become more prominent in search results for relevant keywords. Fail to do that and you may effectively become invisible in search engine results. That puts you out of the race for being short-listed by prospects at the outset of their research journey. We'll look at what "great" content actually looks like a little later.

This change in marketing approach has also required that budgets are re-engineered. Modern marketing requires a smaller budget for traditional media, but a larger budget for the production and management of content in an integrated way across multiple digital platforms; websites, YouTube, Facebook, Twitter, Instagram, apps, Pinterest, and so on. You may not use them all; instead you can employ your persona and customer journey mapping work to reveal which are the most valuable. It also helps to get smarter at re-purposing content in various formats to suit each channel and make your investment in content work harder.

Customer relationship management

[Customer relationship management: an organisation's proactive interaction with its customers or audiences.]

It often takes considerable time and effort to acquire new customers, but they can be lost in a moment. The most successful businesses have always treated loyalty as a natural consequence of a great customer experience, not just a way to keep customers on the hook. Building customer advocacy is central to their long-term business strategy. CRM is, of course, based on the tried and tested commercial truth that it's cheaper to keep existing customers than it is to find new ones. As we all know, acquiring customers is a resource-intensive business.

But I have been frequently surprised how few resources SMEs tend to devote to maintaining and developing relationships with their customers. Many seem to go through the motions, happy that they are sending a regular email to customers, without thinking too much about what's in that email and how relevant it is to their various audience segments.

It's worth taking on board the following rules of thumb:

- Acquiring a new customer will cost anywhere from five to twenty-five times more than retaining an existing one (*Harvard Business Review*)
- Increasing customer retention by just 5 per cent boosts profits by 25–95 per cent (*Bain & Company*)
- The probability of selling to an existing customer is 60–70 per cent. The probability of selling to a new prospect is 5–20 per cent (according to the White House Office of Consumer Affairs as reported by *Return on Behavior* magazine).

There are, of course, inevitable differences across sectors, markets and product types. Nonetheless, research has consistently shown that working to keep customers and sell more to them, makes very good financial sense. The starting point for building engagement is knowing your customers and being able to use this knowledge to inform the interactions you have with them. Building engagement starts with the process of exchanging information between the customer and the business.

For example, the business might provide the customer with knowledge about products, services and their brand values, while the customer provides information such as their preferences, demographic information or insights into their specific interests from their digital interactions. Over time, this exchange of information increases the accumulated pool of knowledge between both parties, which helps to build trust and turn connections into deeper relationships. More specifically it helps organisations to enhance the value they can provide to their customers by offering more relevant products and services.

Smart businesses understand that their integrated customer database is their most important asset. The objective should be to have a complete "single view" of a customer. This requires the creation of a data warehouse, into which a customer's data is fed from all customer touchpoints. You can learn a lot about prospects during their research phase. Perhaps the guides or reports they download, the products they look at or other content they view on the website they visit. Hopefully, you have created compelling reasons for them to give you their email address so that you can then use this information to convert them to a customer. Post-purchase, you have their transaction history, which allows you to form a more detailed picture of them, one that perhaps includes age, gender and other demographic data.

CRM propositions vary depending on the type of organisation. But the driving factor behind all of them is a commitment to understanding audiences, supported by relevant communications, customer service and the intelligent analysis of data. Central to CRM is an understanding of Customer Lifetime Value" (CLTV), the value a customer has to the organisation, in net profit terms, over a period of time. When you understand what the average CLTV of customers is, you know how much you can afford to spend on acquiring them, and that is an important source of competitive advantage.

You will also gain an understanding of who your best customers are, so that you can prioritise efforts to keep them on board. The customer may always be right, but they are not all of equal value. Some will be worth a bigger CRM investment than others. In practise, that means applying lighter-touch techniques, such as automated email communications for the majority of customers, in order to free up resources to do more for the more valuable few.

Today, marketing people should be as comfortable with spreadsheets as the financial director. At a minimum they need to understand how much it costs, on average, to acquire a new customer and relate that to the average revenue and margin you make from them. When you sell online, with the ability to track a prospect through to purchase, you can make a calculation about the success of your marketing. You can determine your return on marketing investment. You can work out how much, on average it actually costs to acquire a new customer and measure that against the amount you should be spending to get them.

Whatever your industry or business model and whether you are B2B or B2C, you need to understand your allowable cost per acquisition (ACPA). It is arguably the most important metric in marketing, and the one that most profoundly affects the bottom line. It informs every aspect of your marketing economics and media strategy. It is the number against which you measure your actual acquisition cost performance.

Marketeers should share a common objective: to obtain an *actual* cost per acquisition (CPA) that is equal to or lower than our ACPA. Together with the ACPA, the CPA is a fundamental KPI for most organisations, as it is all about return on investment and profit. You need to know which individual channels and mix of channels are delivering the best customer volumes and CPAs, so that you maximise the impact of your marketing budget.

That takes us back to CLTV. For example, when you are competing for visibility in the paid search auction, you may be able to bid higher if you know that your average CLTV is greater than a single purchase average order value. In other words, you can attract more new customers by outbidding your competitors because you know that on average you will make an acceptable return based on *all the purchases* an average customer makes over a period, rather than calculating ROI on a single transaction.

Of course, many businesses generate offline purchases from their digital marketing activity. That's okay if it happens through a customer contact centre. Today, we can track from advert and search engine to purchase over the phone or via email. It gets trickier if you also sell through physical shops, but even then, there are ways and means of tracking back to spend on specific digital channels.

When you know and understand these metrics, tracked by free or low-cost tools, you can make constant adjustments to ensure that your marketing budget is being spent in the most productive areas. As with most digital activities, it's all in the set-up. Those who take the time to get their tracking set up properly will reap the benefits in cutting out wasted spend. They can then redirect budget into more financially rewarding marketing opportunities.

We now need our marketeers to be accountable and comfortable with the maths that comes with that accountability. It's left brain stuff. But the right side of a modern marketeer's brain remains as important as ever. This is the creative side that helps them to develop compelling narratives, propositions, messaging and ideas to attract and retain customers. We'll come back to the importance of creativity shortly.

[Left and right brain hemispheres: the left side of the brain is responsible for controlling the right side of the body. It also performs tasks that have to do with logic, such as in science and mathematics. On the other hand, the right hemisphere co-ordinates the left side of the body and performs tasks that have do with creativity and the arts.]

All this means that your marketing people need a whole new skill set, which I call "whole brain marketing". They need a deeper knowledge of their audience so that they can take advantage of more precise ways to use digital marketing to target prospects. They need to understand the often complex customer journey and they need a working knowledge of website usability, technology and tracking.

They also need to understand the marketing maths and to turn data into actionable insights. They need to be flexible and agile in the way they work, able to collaborate effectively with all functions within the organisation, with a test and learn mindset. That's on top of knowing the ins and outs of each digital channel, from email to social media, with the ability to understand how each can play a tactical role in delivering the strategy. To deliver results they also need to understand which technical tools they need and how to use them. All this in addition to traditional marketing creativity.

That's quite a heavy job description and is one that requires energy, experience, curiosity and plenty of both left and right brain thinking. If you're serious about growth, it's not a role for the new intern who knows a bit about social media.

Need-to-know workout tips: six modern marketing focus areas

Let's summarise what business leaders need to know about modern marketing:

1   Content (aka inbound) marketing: it makes great commercial sense because it pulls clients to you when they are ready to buy or at least engage with the buying process. It requires a different resourcing approach compared to traditional outbound campaign marketing; namely, an increased budget to create high-quality content to *earn* attention rather than media cost to *buy* it.
2   Always-on marketing: traditional campaign marketing needs to be blended with always-on marketing. Target and nurture prospects throughout their research, engagement and buying journey across paid, owned and earned media – the sales funnel.
3   Marketing as a dialogue: marketing has moved from one-way broadcast marketing to conversations with audiences. People no longer simply want to consume content. They also like to produce, share and review, using multiple devices such PCs, tablets and smartphones. Data capture, analysis and customer relationship management should be prioritised.
4   Test and track: digital marketing is fast to deploy and easy to track. This means that you can test and optimise different marketing ideas quickly and cheaply, providing the opportunity to improve as you go. Sales are precisely tracked back to the mix of marketing activity used to generate them, so that return on investment is visible.

5   Audience and customer knowledge: this is now more important than ever because you can target more accurately, whether through the use of social media's in-depth demographic targeting, contextual marketing or simply knowing the keywords that your best customers use. Customer knowledge increases your relevance, targeting and ultimately your ROI.
6   Doing the numbers: understand the direct marketing mathematics of your customer acquisition and retention activity.

Digital selling

The memorably named sales expert Zig Ziglar said that "Every sale has five obstacles: no need, no money, no hurry, no desire, no trust." These obstacles need to be overcome in the digital marketplace, just as they are in face-to-face selling environments. Therefore, in addition to those digital marketing skills, a modern marketeer must also be an effective sales person.

People who have sold successfully are, in my experience, much better marketeers. They know how to engage with people and turn them into sales opportunities. Great sales people have to do several things very well. They need to be good at reading people and quickly reach an understanding of their motivations and influences. They can use this empathy to adapt their style, develop a good rapport, deepen the relationship, and build – that word again – trust. They need to be persuasive, persistent and good at closing sales. If we translate those things into a digital business context, we can break them down into six elements:

1   Usability

[Usability: the degree to which software can be used by specified consumers to achieve quantified objectives with effectiveness, efficiency and satisfaction in a quantified context of use.]

Put more simply, usability is essentially about designing a user interface on your app or website that helps customers to find information and accomplish tasks quickly, easily and, ideally, pleasurably. It's an important part of the overall customer experience, an opportunity to develop a relationship and make it easy for people to research and buy.

Assuming that you are attracting click-throughs from qualified prospects, you then need to ensure that your website is persuasive. It needs to create a strong first impression, with content, functionality and design that tells your story and positions your offer effectively. Ultimately, usability seeks to reduce the noise for the user of a website or app; to make it easier for people to consume content, understand the offer and take action, using whatever device they choose.

If users are confronted with too much information or poor navigation they can become confused and unsure what to do next. They are probably in a hurry and can quickly lose faith in whoever it is that's making life more difficult for them. The usability of an organisation's website or app therefore has a deep impact on brand perception as well as conversion.

2   Personalisation

Closely linked to usability is personalisation; this is the *reading people* part of the sales process, ensuring that your content on websites and in emails is responsive to the specific needs of each individual prospect. In today's marketplace personalisation matters. A study by Accenture Interactive in 2016 found that 75 per cent of consumers are more likely to buy from a retailer that recognises them by name, serves up recommendations based on past purchases, or acknowledges their purchase history.

There is personalisation and *personalisation*. In its simplest form you have segment-based personalisation, creating relevant content for each of your customer personas. At the more sophisticated end of the spectrum it's called contextual marketing, which involves presenting content and propositions to an individual prospect based on their previous actions and their location in the customer journey.

Contextual marketing is effectively the art and science of creating meaningful interactions with people, based on who they are and what they do, continuously over time, often in real time. It's a powerful conversion driver, making it easier for prospects to act as they get the information they need to take decisions faster. But the operational reality of advanced personalisation isn't easy at all. It requires the integration of multiple platforms, a bespoke customer data platform and often a dash of data science.

The majority of marketeers have customer data spread across a surprising number of databases. This creates challenges in developing a single view of the customer and makes co-ordinating marketing across channels difficult.

A contextual marketing engine is made up from a number of elements. You need tools such marketing automation software, real-time analytics and customer databases. But you also need personalised content to deliver contextually throughout the customer journey. It is the next step for SMEs in digital sales and marketing, and effectively bridges the gap between marketing and customer experience. But you should approach this kind of deep personalisation with your eyes wide open.

For most SMEs there is much that you can do to improve relevance without going the whole hog to real-time personalisation. As with all digital execution, you should get your sales basics done first before considering a major investment of this kind. That includes ensuring that you have clear and persuasive messaging and prominent calls to action on your website and in your marketing collateral. Those are your sale "closers". It also includes the creation of multiple landing pages that greet new visitors to your website. These web pages must be designed with content and propositions that are directly relevant to the context of the link visitors clicked, either on another website or by entering keywords into a search engine.

3   Offer

You may also need a compelling offer that makes it easier for your prospects to make the decision to buy – perhaps a free trial, free delivery, a clear refund policy or other free extras if they "buy now". It's about encouraging buyers to take action there and then, with all mental obstacles removed.

There are many ways to nudge consumers into taking action on your website, beyond the "buy now" call to action. You can create limited time offers or create a sense of urgency by showing sold out products or that availability is limited. These techniques won't be right for everyone and must be ethically executed, but are used to great effect by travel, retail and ticketing websites the world over.

4   Influencers

That may still be not enough to get the sale though. People will look for evidence that your product or service is as good as you say it is, and that you keep your promises. That means social proof from customers and industry influencers. These influencer websites or blogs are likely to have good search engine visibility for search terms that you may not rank highly for, and therefore may have potential as an affiliate or other type of commercial partnership.

[Affiliate marketing: a type of performance-based marketing in which a business rewards one or more affiliates for each visitor or customer brought by the affiliate's own marketing efforts.]

For some SMEs it can also be important to review how influencers are affecting prospect behaviour at various points in the buying process for a product or service. There are essentially three types of influencer content: credible experts; third-party articles; and user-generated content reviews. All three content types have a role, but expert content is arguably the most influential. Most consumers regularly seek out expert content for products they are considering.

Customer reviews are also crucial to digital selling. Your prospects are looking for social proof to reassure themselves they are making a good purchasing decision. They want to know that people like them have approved your product and service, so that they can weigh these opinions against your claims as the seller.

But you need to work at it. As part of one project I led for a specialist travel company, we emailed every past customer and asked them if they would be willing to provide us with a review of the tour they took. We gave them four specific questions to answer, and the response was astonishingly high and positive. In just a couple of weeks we secured hundreds of great reviews and conversion rates on tours with relevant reviews increased substantially.

5 Remarketing

[Remarketing (aka retargeting): a way of connecting with visitors to your website who may not have made an immediate purchase or enquiry. It allows you to position targeted ads in front of a defined audience that have previously visited your website as they browse elsewhere on the internet.]

A good sales person is also persistent, without being pushy. They understand that there may be interest in the product they are selling but the timing might be off. Digital retargeting, those adverts that follow you around online after you visited a website (and collected a cookie), work on the same principle.

There are several types of retargeting, but the principle behind each remains the same. That is, if you visit an organisation's website you are demonstrating some level of interest in the products or services they offer. You may not make a purchase on that visit for any number of reasons. Perhaps you have simply run out of time; you may have a meeting to get to, or it's time for the school run.

Perhaps it's a more considered purchase and you're simply doing your due diligence to compare features, benefits and price from various suppliers. Or maybe you want to buy but don't have your payment details to hand, or you've run into a problem with the website through the checkout process.

Whatever the reason, you have become a hot prospect for that organisation and it makes sense for them to follow up with you to see if they can nudge you into buying. That ability to nudge is made much easier if you have given the merchant your email address. This may be because you have requested some further information, perhaps a guide to something, or created a wish list or entered it as part of a checkout process that you then abandoned.

The organisation can then send you a follow-up email, or a sequence of automated emails (aka "prospect cycle") to try and secure a sale. But don't forget that if you're operating within the European Union you will need to ensure that your cookie policy is General Data Protection Regulation (GDPR) compliant and that you have express permission from the prospect to send them emails.

6   Conversion rate optimisation

Putting it all together creates a digital conversion funnel (aka sales funnel), something that you're always working to improve through the ongoing activity of conversion rate optimisation (CRO).

[Conversion funnel: a phrase used to describe the journey a consumer takes via a website to becoming a customer. The metaphor of a funnel is used to describe the way in which users are guided to their goal with fewer navigation options at each step.]

A sales funnel refers specifically to the digital process that a consumer goes through on your website to make a purchase – from arriving on a landing page, to finding and selecting products to add to their cart, to checkout and finally order confirmation. As we have seen, this may not all happen within a single session, as users may stop, before returning later to finish a transaction. Defining the steps of your sales funnel will help you to better understand where there are issues in the buying process. It is part of the wider customer journey analysis; together they provide the complete picture of why and how a customer bought your product/service.

Think of CRO as honing your sales skills over time, improving your close rate gradually as you learn more about what your customers really like and want. Small improvements can make a big difference. The rule of thumb is "simplify, simplify, simplify" – particularly as customers narrow their product selection through the process.

The main principles of CRO are:

- Use the analytics as a starting point to understand the biggest weaknesses in the conversion funnel.
- Use testing experiments to continually test, track, learn and improve.

After all that effort you may get a digital sale or a new client. It's been hard work and, without analytics, largely invisible to the naked eye. Perhaps that's why it's easy to forget how hard it is to win a new customer online. We can't see them browsing in our shop, coming up to the till or just walking out. We haven't had that face-to-face or telephone conversation with them. We need to constantly use our analytics tools to see what's going on below the surface so that we can act appropriately to maximise our sales performance. That's why analytics tops the modern marketing "stack" (see Figure 10).

Some organisations still insist on a "churn and burn" approach to business – the commercial equivalent of a one-night stand – rather than work to develop a lasting relationship. There are occasional benefits to churn. For example, it can help companies to get rid of the less profitable but more demanding customers sooner rather than later. But as a business philosophy it is deeply flawed in a number of respects in the digital marketplace.

It's madness to invest marketing resources in driving traffic to your website and to then spend little or no resource on developing that relationship to ensure that you turn them, at some stage, into customers. It's relatively low cost (by conversion funnel optimisation, email or remarketing) and highly effective in driving up your overall conversion rate.

If you don't, you are effectively saying that if a visitor doesn't buy on the first visit to your digital platform then forget 'em. That's clearly absurd. In the travel industry, for example, it can often take more than thirty contacts before someone buys a holiday, as they go back and forth researching and considering options, before seeking approval from the rest of their travelling companions. For most purchases it won't be that many, but very few people take the decision to buy on their first visit online.

It is therefore essential that you develop a marketing approach that helps to nurture those valuable leads, so that you can encourage and nudge prospects towards making a purchase. In the digital world it really helps to build up a fan base. Think reviews. Think social media. Think reputation and think trust. Your customers can become your best marketeers if you have invested in developing a relationship with them, built on the strong foundations of a great product of course, but also by showing that you actually care.

Conversely, the churn attitude, which at its heart implies a disregard for customers, can easily lead to the opposite, a hate base. If you have a business model where the barriers to entry are very high and you consistently deliver on your core product promise, you may be successful with a kind of "treat them mean and keep them keen" approach. I'm sure we can all think of examples. But for the vast majority of businesses this is not a recipe for success.

It doesn't mean that you need to metaphorically take your customers on a five-star trip to Paris. Relationships are cemented by the little things that show you really care. Loyalty can be a fickle thing in the transparent world of digital, where competitors are just a click away, but it still counts for a lot. Encouraging and nurturing loyalty makes good commercial sense when you upsell, cross-sell and benefit from repeat purchases.

In a digital marketplace, a little more conversation is seldom wasted. Love at first sight is increasingly rare. People can now get a much broader view of their options. Selling yourself requires effort in nurturing; wooing, if you like. It's really quite romantic, despite being described in a particularly unromantic way – that "sales funnel" I referred to earlier – in the trade. What isn't romantic is being constantly stalked, pestered and pitched to at every opportunity. It's much better to build up trust over time and get to know one another better. The more you know and share, the closer you get. So, slow down the hard sell and you might get into a deeper relationship that proves more rewarding in the long run.

Figure 10 shows how the elements of a modern marketing "stack" come together:

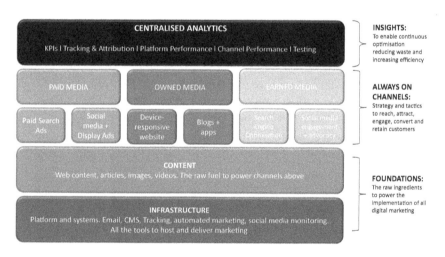

Figure 10 A modern marketing stack

Creative skills

The word creativity doesn't always spring to mind in the context of digital transformation. But it should. The opportunity for human creativity has been increased enormously by technology. Mechanisation over the last 100 years or so has vastly increased our leisure time as well as our incomes.

Arguably the greatest labour-saving device has been the domestic washing machine, which has emancipated us from the drudgery of doing laundry by hand. The machines have set us free to do more interesting things in our personal and working lives.

For me, that's the really exciting opportunity of digital transformation. It has the potential to help organisations to streamline and automate the escalating number of work tasks that a digital world demands, so that they create space to be more creative and responsive to customers. That is playing to the strengths of technology and freeing up humans to play to theirs.

Many business commentators take the view that creativity is the defining characteristic of developed twenty-first-century economies, just as manufacturing typified the nineteenth and early twentieth centuries. After all, the root of differentiation in an increasingly commoditised world is creativity – it helps you to stand out from the herd.

Creativity is not just about having great ideas, but also the ability to execute them. Being able to communicate a message properly is extremely important. As customers, our heads can be convinced by persuasive copy and our hearts won over by visuals that pull on our emotional strings. So, every organisation needs to get better at telling their story, because humans still connect with them as they have since time immemorial. Stories help people to relate and become engaged. Such stories can be about the difference you made to a customer or the unique properties of a product. Or they can be about staff, their passion, experience, commitment and training.

Tell those stories in video, blogs or images, keeping them simple and authentic. Make your story more compelling than those of your competitors. Ultimately, that's what differentiates strong brands from the also-rans.

Specialist skills

Once you're clear about the skills you need, the next question is, do you need people who know a lot about a little – or a little about a lot? Clearly, larger businesses have the capacity for more specialists. They might have experts in search engine marketing, content, CRM, social media, analytics, customer experience, digital usability and conversion rate optimisation. They may also have in-house web developers.

Of course, smaller businesses need generalists; people who see the bigger picture and understand how a mix of all the specialties can contribute to delivering business objectives. Generalists may be required to manage external agencies, whereas specialists are required for in-house work.

As organisations grow, they will need more specialists. But it's not enough for employees to be great at their specialisms. They need to be good team players too. The best results come from hiring the best talent and ensuring that they can work within a driven and collaborative team ethic.

It's important that digital staff can grasp the brand and the creative ideas, so that that they are able to execute them in a technical way.

In other words, they must be able to embrace both the art and the science of digital business. They need to be *cross-fit* so that they have an all-round understanding of functions within their organisation, as well as a deep understanding of their own specialities. Most of all, they need to be customer focused as well as commercial.

In-house skills

Leaders need to weigh the activities that should be undertaken in-house as opposed to those that are best outsourced. You need to consider what outsourcing is appropriate from both productivity and cost-efficiency perspectives. This thinking should also encompass strategic considerations. For example, you may want to build capability in-house because you will get more long-term value from that. Perhaps your business has a significant dependency on search engine traffic, in which case it could be more cost-effective to have someone working in-house on SEO, rather than paying agency fees. A web developer may be required less often than a data analyst. It all depends on your present circumstances, future plans and priorities.

Whatever your scale and level of digital business fitness, the important thing is to evolve, so that, although you may always use agencies and other freelance specialists, you work to develop the capability of your internal team over time. That will foster a deeper understanding of, and closer collaboration on, the many moving parts of your digitally powered business machine.

Practical steps need to be taken to ensure that the increased workload can be managed without increasing resource costs to unsustainable levels. That requires careful planning to ensure that you have the right skill sets, using a combination of in-house resources, external agencies and freelancers as you grow.

Let's go back to marketing as our example. For decades, marketing was largely focused on the delivery of campaigns. That's what marketing departments, working with advertising agencies, mainly did. But now marketing has shifted from a campaign-driven approach to an always-on, inbound marketing emphasis. Because it is "always on", inbound marketing must be process-driven, with activities embedded in the day-to-day work of a marketing department.

In addition to the management of paid search and social media activity, daily tasks will include content creation and deployment. It all needs good co-ordination to ensure that all the elements of your digital marketing mix – people, platforms and marketing strategy – work well together.

From a marketing perspective, my rule of thumb would be that you should undertake always-on, inbound marketing using internal resources if you possibly can and outsource outbound campaign marketing to good agencies.

Soft skills

It is becoming increasingly clear that many of the tasks now performed by humans at work will be undertaken by machines in the future. If the tasks are physical they will be performed by robots, but if they are cognitive, they will be done using AI or a kind of bionic human-machine hybrid.

But, for the foreseeable future at least, it is unlikely that machines will become adept at reading a person's mood or developing deep relationships. It's our soft skills that make us the human counterbalance to the heartless technology. So, as argued in the World Economic Forum report, *The Future of Jobs*, it is human "soft skills" that will become increasingly valuable – skills such as empathy, context sensing, collaboration and creative thinking. I've already covered creativity, so let's look at some of the other soft skills leaders will need to look for in their teams.

Fully formed, perfect employees, like perfect leaders and hens' teeth, are in short supply. But we should aim high. Successful organisations are driven by open-minded teams and individuals, who are always ready to accept the latest technology and make it work for the business. They tend to see challenges as opportunities rather than threats.

Like their leaders they must possess a growth mindset. The constantly changing nature of digital business requires professionals to continually update their skills and work on their personal development. Learning about new tools, platforms and techniques is just one of the reasons why people shouldn't get bored of their jobs.

Organisations also need people who can communicate effectively. So much of what drives success comes down to effective communication. They need to be good at organising their thoughts and presenting their ideas. But they must also be very good listeners who are not constantly on transmit. "We have two ears and one mouth so that we can listen twice as much as we speak", said the Greek philosopher Epictetus. It's good advice. Most of us would do well to listen more to our customers and colleagues, particularly those closest to the front line.

For organisational structures to become less reliant on hierarchy and more on individual empowerment and autonomy, as doing business more digitally requires, organisations need their people to be more self-reliant. So common sense, initiative and an ability to troubleshoot are key attributes to look for in potential employees. Most of all, look for positive and playful people. You know the saying: if you want to provide good service, hire nice people. Or, as Charles Koch put it: "When hiring, if forced to choose between virtue and talent, choose virtue".

Talent management skills

Business leaders talk a lot about their people being their most important asset. How successful you are at finding, developing and retaining talented people can make or break a business. In the digital space, the battle for top talent has always been fierce, particularly as more and more organisations recognise that digital is now core competency stuff, no longer the bit on the side that can be simply be farmed out to agencies.

The fast-paced expansion of digital has led to demand outstripping supply across a number of skill sets. This is compounded by the further specialisation of roles, meaning that competition is getting tougher. It's a sellers' market for digital skills and will be for some time. That's not because of a scarcity of digital natives, but because of a shortage of people who have the commercial experience and people skills to put those digital skills to the best possible use.

This talent grab has led to a significant shift in tone from HR functions. Recruitment is now about emphasising the organisation's culture and work environment, as well as the remuneration. It's important to be attractive and ensure that your HR department is marketing your business effectively to potential employees. With this in mind, there is a lot you can do as a leader to create an attractive picture of your organisation as a place to work. You will need a strong social media presence and positive PR to attract the brightest and the best.

If you have attracted and developed talented people, you will want to hold on to them. That means keeping your team happy and well rewarded. I'm not just talking about money, although making sure that you offer competitive packages is important.

For a new generation of employees, it's about working in an environment where they feel that their contribution is visible and recognised; a place where they can develop, where they share the company's values and are valued. That funky workspace with AstroTurf flooring and table football may help to attract some of those people. But you'll need a healthy culture that is more *real* to stop them looking for even greener grass elsewhere.

Digital specialists tend to want to work for digitally mature companies because they allow employees to improve their productivity and further develop their digital skills. They also want to have access to all the tools of their trade. We talk about customer experience a lot, and rightly so, because we know that customers won't adopt digital services that aren't easy to use. But we also need to think about our employee experience.

Organisations can also differentiate themselves and attract more talent by being open to different ways of working. According to a 2018 YouGov study, only 6 per cent of people in the UK now work a traditional nine-to-five day. Almost half of people work flexibly, job sharing or working compressed hours, allowing them to juggle other commitments. Flexibility is desired by workers of all life stages and ages, and those who do work flexibly reported that they are more motivated, and it encourages them to stay in a job for longer.

It's also vital to develop the talent you have, ensuring that capable people can move into roles that are more relevant for a digital and multichannel world. Some time ago I was hired to lead a digital transformation at one of the world's top galleries. It was at a time when annual digital visitors had exceeded physical visitors for the first time. Their financial position had been affected by a reduction in government subsidy and therefore there was recognition among directors that the organisation had to become more commercial and digitally focused.

Their transformation had many components, one of which was an organisational restructure of the marketing communications department, designed to refocus the team on the new priorities and ways of working. There was naturally considerable unease about this process among those directly affected, particularly as I had communicated that some roles would need to go to make room for some new ones.

However, as we moved through the process that unease largely turned into enthusiasm, as it became clear that many of those whose roles were at risk were very qualified and well motivated to take up the new roles. In fact, several were better qualified for the new roles than for their existing jobs, particularly when given some training to cover any capability gaps.

This was only discovered because we took the time to identify the transferable skills and passions of the people affected. We did not want, nor needed to lose, valuable team members; we simply needed them to do different things – things that they understood needed to be done in a digital world and were excited about doing. It is, of course, not always as simple as that. Sometimes people don't want to change or lack the relevant transferable skills. But I have learned it often pays to dig a little deeper and rein in assumptions.

Finally, leaders of SMEs should make full use of the army of self-employed digital specialists to grow their operations, while keeping fixed costs down. Increasingly, SMEs have a business model based on a relatively small group of core full-time employees, working with a larger number of freelancers or contractors. They are tapping into a national and international talent pool, rather than limiting themselves to those within a reasonable daily commute.

Component 4: Power

Figure 11 Power six-pack

Power of the cloud

Once you've built the capability in terms of skills you can start to put the power down – the superhuman power all businesses need in ultra-competitive digital marketplaces. Think of people and technology platforms working together as your bionic business muscle groups – the organisational biceps, triceps and quads that help you to do the heavy lifting and get things done effectively and efficiently.

[Cloud computing: a way of delivering IT services in which resources are retrieved from the internet ("the cloud") through web-based tools and applications, as opposed to a direct, local connection to a server.]

While some have had their heads in the clouds, others have put their systems there. It's no exaggeration to say that the cloud is redefining the way organisations of all sizes do business. We all use cloud computing every day, even if we don't always know it. When we use any online service to send emails, edit documents, stream movies and music, play games, or store pictures and other files, it's probable that cloud computing is making it all happen behind the scenes. Accessing software applications through the internet, rather than from physical computers sitting in the office, has become the technology game changer.

Put simply, cloud computing means that enterprises shift the delivery of computing services such as servers, storage, databases, networking, software, analytics, and so on to the internet. Companies offering these computing services are called cloud providers and typically charge for services based on usage, in a similar way to gas or electricity at home.

There is a lot of understandable confusion around the terminology of cloud computing, not helped by many of the vendors themselves using terms interchangeably. Most cloud computing services fall into three broad categories: Infrastructure as a Service (IaaS), Platform as a Service (PaaS) and Software as a Service (SaaS). I won't get into all the ins and outs of each because you didn't sign-up for an IT lecture.

What business leaders really want to know is what the benefits of cloud computing are. Essentially, the key benefits are cost, flexibility, security and scalability – and the relative ease of adoption and integration. Let's take a look at each of these, as well as some other benefits, in a bit more detail.

1   Cost

Cloud services reduce costs in a number of ways, and not just through efficiency and productivity gains. A significant benefit of the cloud for smaller businesses is that they no longer have to worry about large upfront IT costs or costly software upgrades. A business IT infrastructure used to be very physical thing in many SMEs. There were lots of plastic boxes and wires everywhere, particularly in the little data centre room, which hummed away as a stack of servers did their thing. When something went wrong the IT crowd would wearily sort it out before moving on to sort out the next mini-emergency.

The expense of that approach, until recently the only game in town, could quickly rack up; the cost of round-the-clock electricity for power and cooling, the cost of the kit and the cost of IT specialists managing the infrastructure. The investment in acquiring and maintaining the physical IT infrastructure was a significant overhead of running a business, taking a large percentage of a company's budget, whatever its scale. Today, that all seems a bit Stone Age compared to the modern cloud environment. By migrating to the cloud, organisations can avoid many of those upfront and ongoing costs.

2   Ease of adoption and integration

For smaller businesses in particular, those savings are invaluable. It gives them access to software that may be cost-prohibitive on a more traditional delivery model. It effectively makes the kind of technology that only the likes of Amazon would have had access to a few years ago accessible to almost everyone.

Adopting a cloud-based business solution also creates multiple opportunities for the simplified integration of back office operations, from HR to marketing to accounting. These opportunities for closer integration give small business leaders more time to focus on the more critical areas of their operations.

3   IT productivity

Having your own IT infrastructure entails a lot of what IT pros call "racking and stacking". That is hardware set-up, software patching and other time-consuming IT management chores. Cloud computing removes the need for many of these tasks, freeing up human resources for other more profitable activities.

4   Scalability

The fact that they can grow with the business is another advantage of cloud applications. The cloud is completely scalable, meaning that vendors can deliver the right amount of IT resources - for example, more or less computing power, storage and bandwidth – precisely when it's needed. It enables an organisation to increase and decrease the number of system users, depending on current business needs and the number of employees. That really takes the pressure off capacity planning.

It doesn't have to happen all at once. An organisation may begin with cloud applications such as database, email and website, before progressing to a fully integrated cloud strategy as it picks up experience with, and confidence in, the cloud.

5   Flexibility

As the world becomes increasingly mobile, a key benefit of the cloud is being able to access files and information from any device in any place at any time. It's becoming hard to remember when files were stuck on a single computer and the days of USB flash drives are numbered.

Of course, this is becoming increasingly important as modern businesses use remote workers and offer flexible working arrangements. Not only does cloud computing make it easier for employees to work outside of the office, it makes it easier for business leaders to stay connected at any time and from anywhere. Productivity will be boosted when you enable your people to work from any place and on whatever device they choose, particularly when you have a smaller workforce who can't be everywhere at once.

6   Collaboration

Such flexibility means that collaboration is made much easier by the cloud. It can be simple things like enabling employees to easily work from the same master document. Or it can be the use of more sophisticated collaboration tools that enable the efficient sharing of documents and facilitate the tracking and management of projects and other critical business activities.

7   Security

Security is another advantage. We all know that cyber security is now a very big issue. Over half of all offences recorded in the UK are categorised as cybercrime. Apart from the obvious benefit of having expert security know-how available to the cloud vendors, compared to that in your office, it also helps businesses competing for contracts where security is a key factor. A good example is public sector contracts that insist suppliers work within a government-accredited infrastructure. Often, they will be able to simply buy into a cloud which has already earned the necessary accreditation and they're ready to go.

But there will always be a need for businesses, of any size, to maintain their security vigilance on the ground. Humans in the office are usually the weak link in the security chain. Nevertheless, cloud services can substantially reduce the burden of security.

8   Performance

Cloud computing services offer the kind of performance that most businesses would be unable to emulate using their own infrastructure. They run on a worldwide network of secure data centres, which are regularly upgraded to the latest generation of fast and efficient computing hardware.

9   Reliability

We all know that IT can go wrong, and when it does you need to be properly prepared. Cloud computing makes data back-up, disaster recovery and business continuity easier and less expensive, because data can be mirrored at multiple sites on the cloud provider's network.

All that adds up to a pretty strong case. So, it makes a lot of sense for all leaders to get their heads in the cloud and understand the opportunity. The modern office can now be freed from the many plastic boxes and wires. As long as there is a good internet connection, still sadly not always a given everywhere, employees can be equipped with little more than a laptop and yet become more productive than they have ever been.

A great example of how the cloud can enable new operating models is Ignition Law. This fast-growing start-up is challenging the staunchly traditional UK legal sector. The company saw an opportunity to dramatically reduce costs by eschewing the sector's typical glitzy office in a prestige location. The founders realised that there was an untapped supply of lawyers, such as working mothers, who were qualified to carry out high-end work but no longer willing or able to work full-time in highly competitive, pressurised and long hours office environments. The company uses web-based collaboration tools to enable remote and flexible working for all its lawyers, allowing it to substantially undercut the hourly rates of traditional firms. That combination of skills and low overheads has helped it to grow rapidly in the market.

Power tools

Doing business digitally can be demanding. As we've seen, there are a lot of moving parts. Increasingly, efforts to meet the new expectations of connected customers with old clunky technology and manual processes is an exercise in futility. SMEs must use the new breed of applications and make them more integral to the workflow, productivity, decision-making and regulatory compliance of their operations.

You need the right tools for the job. Fortunately, a new generation of cloud-based digital technology can help. The rise of SaaS has opened the door to specialised, often industry-specific platforms that connect and automate many of these processes.

[Software as a service (SaaS): a software licensing and delivery model in which software is licensed on a subscription basis and is centrally hosted. SaaS is typically accessed by users via a web browser.]

For many years, this type of system has been wishful thinking for SMEs. But today the technology has exponentially increased in power while becoming cheaper and much more user-friendly, making many of these self-service platforms practical and cost-effective for even the smallest enterprises.

These systems are typically easy to customise without the need for external support, so today few SMEs should need to involve themselves in the stress and expense of custom-building their systems. They will also help SMEs to get to a point where they no longer need IT specialists to make changes and drive innovations. Modern tools mean that almost anyone can quickly learn to do most of the things likely to be required by SMEs.

Competition in the SaaS market is fierce. In the space of a few years, literally thousands of vendors have popped up offering a bewildering choice of business tools. There are systems for customer and data analytics, CRM, marketing automation, personalisation and prospect targeting, website content management, social media management, ecommerce, paid media management, mobile app management, finance, procurement, supply chain management, HR, and much more.

These tools have changed the game, making what used to be hard easier, and what used to be expensive much cheaper. For example, cloud-based accounting software can now streamline the whole accounting process, making bill payments, invoicing, payroll and tax returns integrated and simple.

Added to that, collaboration tools, video conferencing and messaging apps help to minimise time-consuming physical staff meetings. Put together, these tools can dramatically improve the way SME teams collaborate, communicate and automate their daily tasks, helping all business functions to improve productivity, efficiency and, ultimately, customer experience.

This has become particularly important given the rise of remote working by both staff and freelancers. Having a cloud-based, cross-department platform means that any authorised individual can contribute more easily just by logging into your company's database from any internet-enabled device. This means that everyone can access relevant data, dramatically reducing instances of interdepartmental miscommunication impacting on customer experience. Just make sure you frequently review your basic security protocols, like resetting passwords.

Despite these opportunities, technology is not being used to its full potential by most SMEs. Too often, leaders simply look at cost savings when reviewing new technology, rather than thinking about future-proofing their organisation for digital business. A conservative mindset that focuses solely on the maintenance of current systems is increasingly holding organisations back at a time when the world is becoming increasingly digital. Instead, leaders must shift their mindset, from one of technology as a necessary cost, to one of new business tools as a key driver of competitive advantage and growth.

All these tools rely on SMEs having a good technical infrastructure. For example, good internet connectivity must be a given. Standard broadband won't cut the mustard if you have a team, even a small team, working on multiple applications in the cloud. Connectivity underpins everything in a cloud-centric world.

It's a necessity for the digital future, due to the increase in flexible working, accessing the cloud and the use of VoIP (the transmission of voice and multimedia content over Internet Protocol networks). Speed, security and scalability will be essential to cope with growing business requirements and enable SMEs to stay nimble, flexible and close to the customer.

Many SMEs, unlike most large enterprises, benefit from not having to deal with legacy systems. They can start to adopt new technology from a clean slate. But for others, legacy systems have huge value and proven reliability. Getting fit for digital doesn't necessarily mean that you need to throw out all the old systems. That may be the easiest route for some, but the right solution may be an integration of the known capabilities of existing systems with new tools that will take you to the next level.

Digital in the context of IT can be focused on creating a two-part environment that decouples legacy systems, which support critical functions and run at a slower pace, from those that support fast-moving, customer-facing interactions. In such cases, your digital platform does the bulk of the real-time work while legacy applications remain as your systems of record. Many digitally fit organisations operate with multiple systems in a technology stack and use application programming interfaces (APIs – more on what they are shortly) to integrate them, ensuring a smooth flow of data between the different systems.

The technology tower of power

The next questions are: which tools are appropriate for your specific needs, and do you need a proverbial multi-gym or individual bits of kit from various vendors to power your digital fitness objectives? There is a big push in the industry to bring functionality together within single, all-singing, all-dancing systems. To keep it simple, let's take a look at this in the context of marketing again. Of all the business functions, marketing has perhaps the most to gain from these tools, and marketeers have been the early adopters. Marketing automation applications have already grown into a billion-dollar industry in just a few years and there's room for a lot more growth yet.

[Marketing automation: Marketing automation refers to software platforms and technologies designed for marketing departments and organisations to more effectively market on multiple channels online and automate repetitive tasks.]

Every fifteen years or so, the IT industry has witnessed new developments which have changed the way IT services are delivered to the business end users. After the mainframe era, mini-computing era, personal computer/client-server era and the World Wide Web era, we're now in what many refer to as the fifth wave of corporate IT. This fifth wave comprises social, mobile, analytics and cloud technologies – aka SMAC, which I talked about in earlier in terms of defining "digital". A modern SME technology stack needs to meet the needs of SMAC.

Essentially, there are six elements that provide the bedrock of your digital sales, marketing and customer experience technology stack: a modern content management system (CMS); analytics software; an email marketing platform; CRM software; social media management systems; and, if you sell online, an ecommerce platform. There are many other tools, such as bid management software, that help to manage your paid search and social media advertising, but those six are the technical foundation stones.

There is also a growing number of automated marketing tools that bring a lot of this functionality together into a single system. These systems have a variety of tools that help marketeers to streamline their activities across a number of channels throughout the customer journey to purchase. They are the Swiss Army knives of marketing, supporting lead generation, segmentation, lead nurturing and lead scoring, cross-selling and upselling, customer retention, and marketing ROI measurement.

Three elements sit at the heart of these systems: first, a central marketing database. This is essentially a data warehouse that stores all the detailed marketing data about prospect and customer interactions and behaviours. Second, there is what I think of as the brain of the system – the engagement marketing engine. This where content is created by users and processes are managed and automated. This is what you use to orchestrate communication and conversations with your prospects and customers across multiple channels to ensure that they receive the right messages at the right times.

Finally, there is the analytics engine, which is used to track, test and optimise marketing activity. It's a tool to help marketeers to understand what worked, what didn't, and to identify areas in the sales and marketing process that you can improve in order to increase revenue and ROI.

These tools streamline sales and marketing by replacing high-touch, repetitive manual processes with automated solutions. In other words, it's about using one system rather than many in order to deploy content in a co-ordinated way so that it can be managed and measured more easily. These automated marketing systems can help organisations to create more integrated, efficient and productive communications.

This "all in one" route can be an attractive option for businesses that want a single system with a single point of supplier, support and training. They can be particularly useful for smaller businesses which don't want the added complexity of integrating multiple systems. But they are less flexible if you find you decide you need more powerful functionality in a key area than a single system provides. Having a platform of "separates" allows you to swap or upgrade different elements, as new products or cheaper prices become available over time.

What I call "separates" are often already configured to allow relatively easy integration with other complimentary systems from various vendors. That's huge progress, if like me you remember the time, effort and expense that used to go into getting different systems to play nicely with each other. We used to have lots of systems that sat with their metaphorical arms folded refusing to be civil to other applications. That meant we had to do lots of boring manual processes to connect the dots or undertake complex and expensive integration work.

Things have improved dramatically, largely thanks to APIs. An API is a particular set of rules and specifications that software programs can follow to communicate with other software. In other words, an API is the interface through which you access somebody else's code or someone else's code accesses yours. All leaders really need to know is that it helps different systems to talk to each other. The benefits of relatively easy system integration cannot be understated. It enables people across business functions to access and share data, the glue that joins everything and everybody together.

[Open source: this denotes software for which the original source code is made freely available and may be redistributed and modified.]

This relative ease of integration has also in large part been driven by the use of open source technologies. Despite that, there will still be some work required to join the dots. Therefore, the upsides of pre-integrated, all-in-one systems will outweigh the flexibility benefits for many businesses.

However you go about it, your technology approach must be cloud-hosted, mobile-first and insight-driven to deliver business responsiveness, reduce cost and lay the foundations for the future. Whether you go for all in one, or loosely coupled separates, will depend on your specific needs and the diligence of your requirement gathering process. Figure 12 shows what a modern marketing technology stack should look like for a progressive SME. It is your technology tower of power. Not every SME will necessarily need all of the elements, but most will if they want to survive and thrive in a digital-first business future.

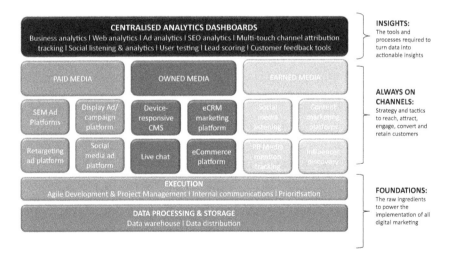

Figure 12 A modern marketing technology stack

Power to choose

It's great that there are so many tools available now to SMEs to help them to improve productivity and customer experience. But leaders still have to figure out which tools to buy and how to use them effectively to boost performance. They can't simply buy a new piece of technical kit and expect it to transform everything on its own.

In my efforts to keep physically fit, I've been as guilty as anyone in purchasing a piece of kit as my get-in-shape silver bullet, buying the promise of "amazing results in just thirty days". I was fooling myself, of course. Deep down I knew that it was never going to be that simple. But I bought it anyway, becoming a paid-up member of the "all the gear and no idea" tribe of the fitness community. Most of this technology soon began the familiar journey from bedroom to attic to charity shop. It wasn't that the kit was bad necessarily. It was just that I didn't choose the right tools for my specific fitness goals or invest sufficient time to learn how to use them properly.

Of course, the same thing happens in business. We look for the technology silver bullet. We're busy and under pressure. That's often when we succumb to the lure of a new bit of kit that promises to solve all our problems. The bottom line is that when you are shopping for new technology or building a new digital product like a website, start from the business problems you are trying to solve, rather than from what the technology seems to offer.

They say that we only use 10 per cent of our brain, which implies that if we could tap into the other 90 per cent we'd have superhuman powers. Well, that's been scientifically disproved. In fact, most of the human brain is active most of the time, and, over the course of each day, you will use just about every part of your brain (particularly if you lead an SME).

But it is true is that businesses consistently buy software and then only use a fraction of the available functionality. There are several reasons for that. It could simply be that someone has bought the wrong piece of kit. Some super sales person has talked somebody in your organisation into buying a Bentley when you really only needed a Volkswagen.

It could also be that the cost of the new bit of kit was so great, especially when combined with the unexpectedly high implementation costs, that there was no budget left to teach your employees how to use it properly. Or possibly the system generates so much data that you simply don't have the resources required to turn that data into the actionable insights that will actually make you more money. Information overload, analysis paralysis – call it what you will.

It's not simply the new bits of kit. Often SMEs fail to make full use of the new technology tools that they have had for some time. These powerful tools can sit there patiently waiting to add value but their capabilities are largely ignored by their human masters. Take something like Google Analytics. It's been available for over a decade now and most businesses have adopted it to track and report activity on their websites.

But, in my experience, very few businesses harness its potential benefits effectively. A business that thinks carefully about what it really needs from analytics, before working to configure Google Analytics to deliver it, is still the exception to the rule. It's a classic example of humans failing to adapt to working with technology in a way that ensures both are delivering to their full potential.

Digital technologies only enable employees to work in different ways; they do not make those actions happen automatically. The act of buying and implementing digital technologies is not sufficient to derive business value from it. Again, an obvious point perhaps, but in my experience, one that's easily overlooked. I've seen many projects that focus almost exclusively on the technical implementation, with little time or resource devoted to the human implications, such as training, capacity, processes and organisational structures.

The number of SaaS vendors runs into the thousands and more are coming onto the market every month. There are tools that help to manage and automate practically every business function. So, how do you make your selection? Don't start with a vendor beauty contest. Begin by making a list of your requirements. Those requirements should emerge from the customer journey mapping exercise that we covered in the "Core strength" section.

That map will show you where the customer pain points are, identifying the touchpoints where the business needs to improve customer experience. It will also inform the conversation about the processes you need to streamline to improve efficiency. On that basis you can then make a list of your requirements, effectively the functionality you think you will need. Then prioritise them, scoring them from one to five.

Next, compile a long list of vendors. There are lots of websites that can help by providing a comparison of features and reviews. Involve your wider team. Discuss the company's objectives and how technology will help to achieve them. Find out how your employees feel about working with these new systems and talk about transition and training requirements.

Functionality is critical, but so is user-friendliness. Technologies that require multiple training days and fat user manuals will understandably generate pushback. Consider running a number of comparative pilots of various technologies to ensure you're choosing the right one. Encourage users to use the free trials that most vendors now offer, using a standard set of criteria to compare performance. Also work to get the actual business users involved early in the selection process. Appoint a "super-user" with a brief to immerse themselves in a new system and understand the pros and cons. Once a piece of software has been adopted, they can provide in-house support to other users and even make video tutorials available to them.

When your long list becomes a shortlist, you can then start getting demos. Keep a gap analysis log to stay on top of what you discover about each system alongside the list of requirements. A simple spreadsheet will do. List all the functionality you think you need, along with the priority score. Then work with the vendor to identify any gaps in functionality for each system you are evaluating. It may be that you discover some "must-have" functionality is missing. You then have to decide whether it really is must-have and, if so, how you can plug that gap, either working with the supplier or integrating other software. That could be time-consuming or expensive. Probably both. So, it may well be better to simply change the way you work to make the enhancement unnecessary.

Power of the team

"It is the long history of humankind (and animal kind, too), that those who learned to collaborate and improvise most effectively have prevailed". Charles Darwin understood the power of teamwork. Quite simply, as Ken Blanchard put it: "None of us is as smart or effective as all of us".

But that is only true if teams are configured appropriately. Simply assembling a group of talented people is not enough because an organisational structure dictates the relationship of roles in an organisation, and therefore, how people function day to day. Organisational-design choices, from the board to the front line can have a profound and lasting effect on company culture.

A company can have a clear vision for digital business, talented people, and great leaders, yet still not perform well because of poor organisational design. When an enterprise's strategy changes, as it must to succeed in a digital world, its structures, roles, and functions should be also be realigned to improve communication, increase productivity and inspire innovation. The grouping of employees in various departments and the managerial hierarchy has a huge influence on the way employees interact with each other on the job.

To be effective, the overall organisation design must be aligned with the business strategy and the market environment in which the business operates. It must also have the right business controls, the right flexibility, the right incentives, the right resources and of course, the right people.

This doesn't always happen, with the result that responsibilities can be overlooked, staffing can be inappropriate, and people, and often whole functions, can work against each other. Too often, outdated organisational design leads to confusion within roles, a lack of coordination among functions and failure to share ideas. This results in slow decision-making, bringing unnecessary complexity, stress, and conflict into the workplace.

The right set-up will vary considerably according to the type and size of your organisation. First of all, leaders need to decide how hierarchical their organisational design should be.

Not very is the answer. Hierarchies create bottlenecks. Bottlenecks stifle speed and agility. A lack of agility is death to digital. (I talk more about this later in the "Agility" section.) Leaders of digital-first organisations recognise the need to simplify their organisation, sweeping away the layers and bureaucracy and developing that all-important culture of shared responsibility.

You will also need to consider your formation in the context of your current level of digital maturity. If you are a good way down the digital track, your objective should be to build digital capability within each individual function of your organisation. Ultimately, that's what all organisations should aim for.

But if you need to need to inject some digital adrenalin into a still largely analogue business, you should consider a short-term "hub" approach. Essentially, this is an autonomous digital function, be it one person or a team, depending on the scale of your organisation and the size of the potential prize. This centre of digital business excellence must have both the skills and the authority to challenge existing ways of working and provide digital solutions that can quickly demonstrate the benefits of change.

At one company undergoing a digital transformation, digital change leaders were known as "dragon slayers". A touch melodramatic perhaps, but they were given a clear remit from the CEO to act fast without having to seek advance approval. They took the heat for bad choices but knew that the one mistake that wouldn't be forgiven was side-stepping the tough decisions in the first place. Not many leaders would be comfortable with that, but if you're on that burning platform, needs must.

For smaller organisations that don't have the resources to hire new full-time digital specialists, the appropriate initial solution may be a digital fitness steering board, made up of existing staff from relevant functions. This approach can succeed if it is led by a seasoned, senior digital leader brought in as an interim or consultant, who has the sponsorship to make things happen. But you will inevitably need some short-term freelance specialists to support implementation.

You will also need to consider where the team actually "sits" both physically and within the organisation chart. Where fast change is required, which is almost everywhere, integrating your digital specialists within an existing IT function can seem attractive. But that may inhibit progress. IT people come in many forms like everybody else, but as a general rule, leaders should be looking for people who think more about customers, communication and connectivity than they think about code.

When I work with a business, one of the first things I like to see is an organisation chart. You can learn a lot about a business from these. In addition to providing an overview of who reports to whom and who is in charge of what, the chart may also tell you something about an organisation's culture. There are hierarchical organisations, which are formal and structured, and there are organic or "ad hoc" organisations, which are more informal and fluid, and evolve as business conditions change.

There is no-one-size-fits-all team formation for a digital business. But, leaders should, as always, try to think differently, considering how the organisational structure can support a digital way of working. As an example, Figure 13 shows a high-level digital sales and marketing team structure that is designed to support the kind of inbound marketing and sales funnel strategy that we looked at earlier.

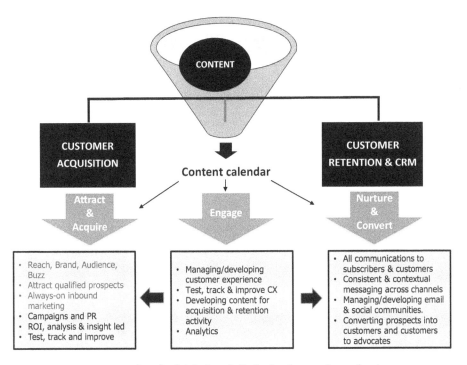

Figure 13 An example of a high-level digital sales and marketing team structure

Power of content

That inbound marketing approach is fuelled by content. High-quality content will increase your visibility in search engines, helping you to attract the right people to your website and build the credibility of your brand. Organisations that understand that they are publishers, as well as product retailers or service providers, prosper if they deploy their content in a way that engages visitors at all stages of the user journey – from stranger to buyer to advocate.

In the context of getting fit for digital business, content should be thought of like nutrition, an important part of your overall health and fitness programme. Good-quality content sustainably fuels the business, helping it to look and perform better. In contrast, poor-quality content simply degrades it. Poor content is like fast food. It's easier, sometimes quicker and often cheaper than more wholesome alternatives, but if you eat it all the time it will eventually lead to health problems. That's why digitally fit enterprises invest in the creation of good nutritious content, rather than churning out fast content, stuffed with keywords, as cheaply as possible.

So, what is "good" content? I would define it as information that is relevant to the reader, listener or viewer, telling them something they didn't know in a way they find interesting. It should communicate new ideas and perspectives. Rule one is that content should be original. The extra effort required to produce useful, engaging content that is genuinely new, rather than a rehash of other people's, pays dividends with search engines as well as with audiences. Google rewards websites that have original content with greater exposure. In fact, it sometimes goes further by actively penalising websites that feature content duplicated from other sources. Human consumers of content are also much more likely to share good, original content, creating links that act like votes to improve your website's standing with search engines.

If you are a retailer, perhaps selling commodity products that many others are selling too, you should also remember that although you need to use standard descriptions (for Google Shopping search results for example), you should consider creating unique descriptive content to help you to stand out from the crowd in the standard search engine results.

An enterprise should focus on producing wholesome content that shows off your knowledge, experience, ideas and area of expertise. There are no short cuts. Anything other than good content is largely a waste of time and resources. It will do little to elevate the perception or visibility of your organisation.

When search engines were less sophisticated than they are today, you could get away with gaming them to rapidly increase your visibility for relevant keywords. The search engine optimisers split into two camps: the "white hats" who concentrated on creating great content that attracted links from other high-quality websites; and the "black hats" who were intent on finding any short cuts they could in order to climb the search engine rankings.

Today, as search engines have become much better at spotting the tricks played on them, "white hat" is the only way to go. But that hasn't stopped the "black hats" toting for business. Organisations can take a big hit by transgressing Google's rules. Over the years there have been several examples of large businesses being penalised for what Google regarded as professional fouls. I know of both a leading car manufacturer and a large insurance company, who some time ago lost tens of thousands of high-quality leads due to, perhaps unknowingly, overstepping the mark. It cost them millions in extra marketing and lost sales, before they were able to recover most of their previous search engine visibility. These businesses had the scale to weather the storm, but SMEs that have become reliant on search as their primary source of business, may not be so resilient.

I was once involved in the acquisition of an online travel agency in the United States, which had built up industry-leading volumes of traffic to their website by adding lots of content to the website and developing deep expertise in SEO. They had become what is known as an "authority site" within their business niche for Google.

In practise, that meant that they were in search result positions one to three for thousands of search terms (aka keywords). But despite having such a large number of website visitors, they weren't actually selling much. In fact, they had begun to make more money from selling advertising on the site than from their core business of selling holidays.

Although they were attracting lots of visitors, increasingly they weren't the right visitors. They were no longer well-qualified prospects and therefore didn't convert to customers. Many of the keywords they were ranking for in search engines were simply too generic. In other words, these visitors were not serious buyers. In fact, in that particular case, a good proportion were actually school children researching answers for their geography homework.

The other issue was that, as sales of advertising became the larger source of revenue, the user experience on the website deteriorated, as advertising took more and more of the website real estate, cluttering the screen and confusing the user. This had a further negative impact on core sales. A split culture began to develop between those whose responsibility it was to sell product, versus those who sold advertising. It went all the way to the top, and the board and investors began to take differing sides on what the primary business model should be. Unsurprisingly, the business began to lose its way.

Then, just as the advertising cheerleaders had all but won the battle, Google implemented a major update to its algorithm, as it tends to do several times a year. This change effectively marked down websites which had a lot of licensed content – copy bought from external suppliers – and marked up websites with more original and unique content.

Almost overnight they lost hundreds of thousands of visitors a month and the advertising model began to look shaky. Unfortunately, by then, the core offer had been undermined; key staff had been laid off; the user experience had been compromised; and a lot of goodwill in the market, from both customers and suppliers, had been lost.

Google's search engine mission is very clear; it needs to give visibility to those websites that provide the best answer to the user's question, as expressed by the keywords they type or dictate into its search box. Google clearly came to believe that websites should not benefit from buying in licensed content that was also available on many other websites. It didn't want to return results from lots of websites with the same duplicate content – and who can argue with that. But that particular business was also the victim of a lack of what we could call strategic integrity, chasing the short-term buck, at the risk of its long-term growth. All this is considerably easier to see with the benefit of hindsight and without factoring in the cash-flow challenges that many growing businesses face.

It's also important to make content stand out from the rest by creating punchy headlines. Many people may read a headline, but only a much smaller number will go on to read the rest, particularly if the title hasn't grabbed their attention. Once you have engaged your reader, be sure to answer the questions that are implied in the headline. It is also useful if you can help your content consumers to easily apply the information you are giving them. That may mean strong calls to action, perhaps to buy or subscribe or simply by summarising how they can best use the lessons in their own business or personal lives.

Most content consumers are looking for answers to questions in some form, and they want to find those answers quickly. So, it makes sense to create content that is easy to scan and that uses good images, diagrams, videos and infographics to get the key points across as engagingly and simply as possible. Remember too that humans are hardwired to respond to stories, so always consider how you can add interest with case studies, anecdotes and analogies to bring content to life in the consumer's mind.

Also keep in mind that the credibility and reputation of your enterprise is on the line when you create content. Ensure that the information you give is accurate, show your sources and review older "live" content to ensure that it's still up to date.

Of course, content is not simply used to pull your audience to you. You will also push content out to your audience, for example in tweets and emails to subscribers. The same rules apply: create original content that is accurate, actionable, scannable and genuinely interesting to your intended audience, with headlines and titles that signal its unique value.

Component 5: Data

Figure 14 Data six-pack

Define

The fifth component of digital fitness is data. Just as fitness trackers measure our heartbeat, digital analytics software tracks our company's pulse and enables us to track the impact of our actions. The old adage "what gets measured gets managed" is more relevant today than ever. It's true that many entrepreneurs have successfully built businesses by trusting their gut instincts. The ability and confidence to act on instinct is a defining characteristic of many leaders. It will endure as an important business trait, of course, just like being lucky.

But in the digital age, a failure to use data effectively for decision-making will put a business at a significant competitive disadvantage. That means that data management is fast becoming a core competency that every enterprise should master but that few, particularly within the SME category, have really nailed so far.

As I said earlier, simply plugging in some standard analytics software and looking at the reports is unlikely to get the job done. You need to do a bit of thinking first and define what you are trying to achieve through your use of data. As always, it really helps to understand where you are starting from, and therefore a data health assessment should form part of your digital business check-up. Figure 15 will help you to assess the current level of data use maturity in your organisation.

There's no point simply picking through data looking for insights. That just wastes time. We need to be a bit more scientific. That means we have to start with a list of specific questions to answer or a hypothesis to investigate. Those questions can't be vague. You don't just want to know how you're performing in a general sense. You want to know how you are doing relative to your SMART objectives – your specific, measurable, achievable, relevant and time-related objectives.

That's not to say that you should ignore the other insights that surface in your data. Just keep your focus firmly on what you set out to accomplish and the data you came for. Getting it right means that an organisation can make faster and more confident business decisions.

You will first need to define your "business as usual" KPIs and metrics, thinking about your data in two broad categories:

1   Performance data: metrics and KPIs on sales, marketing and operational performance.
2   Customer-level data: capturing data that builds your knowledge of each customer so that you can become more relevant, timely and personalised in your marketing and customer service.

Note that although some of these business as usual KPIs may mirror those that you set to track the progress of your digital fitness programme – such as Net Promoter Score – others will reflect more traditional business measures.

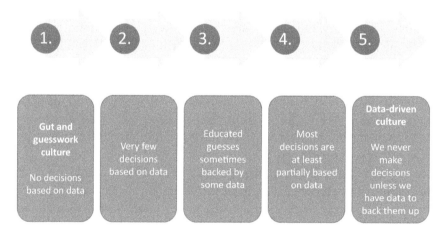

Figure 15 A data use maturity scale

Let's focus on performance data here, as customer data is covered elsewhere in this book. First off, there's a difference between KPIs and metrics. That difference matters. Using them interchangeably creates confusion, and that's bad for business. All KPIs are metrics, but not all metrics are KPIs.

[KPIs versus metrics: a key performance indicator is used to measure performance and success. A metric is simply a number within a KPI that helps to track performance and progress.]

To use a simple example, one of your metrics may be "Monthly Visits" to your website. It's an interesting metric but, in isolation, it doesn't tell you much about your performance. A metric is simply a number. It becomes more useful when you compare it to the same period in previous years or when you combine it with other metrics, such as sales, in order to determine your conversion rate.

KPIs are a small subset of data taken from your metrics, usually derived from a calculation of combined metrics. They show you how you are performing relative to historic performance and targeted goals. KPIs must give you a real insight into your business, creating expectations and driving action. They will include things like revenue, related to targets, of course.

But they will also reflect your strategic objectives. These could be to increase customer acquisition while maintaining an acceptable cost of acquisition, or to improve customer lifetime value. Or they may be your NPS, a measure of your customers' likelihood to recommend your organisation to a family, friends or colleagues. In that case, your KPI would be the *ratio* of positive versus negative sentiment based on a scoring system.

In the context of a digital fitness programme, KPIs can include other measures such as the share of new customers acquired online, or the ratio of budget spent on digital relative to print. Think of KPIs as your business vital signs: the "critical few" key measures of your company's health. Everybody in the organisation should know what these headline indicators are and they should be supported in a logical way by your broader metrics, as these will be required for diagnosis purposes.

So, for example, if one of your KPIs, say the volume of leads from search engine marketing, suddenly takes a big and unexpected drop, you can look at your supporting diagnostic metrics to identify the root cause. It's time well spent to understand the things that are important to measure versus those that aren't. Think about the things you would really love to know under each business area.

Try asking yourselves these questions to get going:

1   What do all stakeholders want to know and why?
2   Which decisions can that data help with?

3   What action will be taken based on this data?

4   How will that action affect the customer and ultimately the bottom line?

5   Have we covered all the bases, e.g. sales and marketing, customer sentiment, operations, production – as well as the usual financial metrics?

6   Which data sources and metrics do we use to derive this information?

7   How do we ensure that this information gives us something reliable to act upon?

8   And how do we communicate this information to different stakeholder groups so that they engage with it appropriately?

Every area of business has specific metrics that should be monitored. Therefore, every business function should play their part in the metrics definition process. Each should measure success based on specific goals and targets, while aligning the overall enterprise strategy and high-level KPIs. But stick to a "critical few".

It helps to have a simple framework for each function. As an example, for marketing I tend to use the RACE framework, defined by Dr Dave Chaffey at Smart Insights, which I have adapted to help organisations to define their metrics and KPIs in terms of Reach, Actions, Conversion and Engagement. It's illustrated in Figure 16.

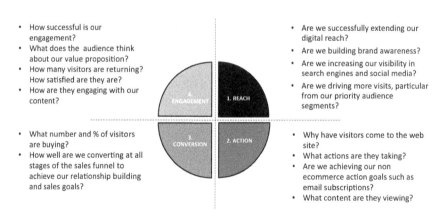

Figure 16 A simple RACE reporting framework

Align

Old school businesses typically develop a culture of "information as power", in the sense that owning data confers higher status within the organisation.

This can lead to power games and the hoarding of data within functional silos, often supported by claims of confidentiality or lack of relevance to other functions. We now live in the information age. Information *is* power. But that power can only be fully deployed if information is available to the many and not the few.

The name of the game today is information sharing, facilitated by a culture that encourages it and digital tools that enable it. The sharing of data enables more people to take rational business decisions faster without having to seek authorisation from further up the chain of command. Data helps to make business as usual operations more transparent, enabling decision-making from anywhere, not just from those on the spot. It helps teams to manage resources more effectively, allowing more resources to be put into things that are working well for the business and reduce resources for activities that are not performing so well, measured against the primary goals.

There may be some data that cannot be disclosed for very good reasons, but as a general rule data accessibility should be strongly encouraged by leaders as a cultural norm, even if the information appears at first sight to be irrelevant. Such easy access and transparency will help to build trust in the data, by lessening opportunities for misinterpretations or biased interpretations. Sometimes we can all be selective about which bits of data to emphasise and which bits we may choose to play down. Leaders need to put systems in place to track data so you, and everybody else, can see exactly what is happening before any gloss is applied.

Being data-driven is not simply about doing analytics or testing or listening to customers. It's about finding the right way to integrate those activities into the everyday thinking and habits of your business. It's not primarily about weekly or monthly reporting, although that has its place. It's more important to ensure that data is easily available to the right people at any time, enabling them to take action quickly, as part of their business as usual routine.

[Business intelligence: (BI) this is defined in the simplest terms as any tool, activity or process used to analyse a company's data to support better decision-making, identify new business opportunities and reduce costs.]

While larger organisations may have the scale to employ dedicated analysts, most SMEs will need to spread access to data across its workforce. For smaller businesses, it's simply not viable to have a full-time staff member dedicated solely to business intelligence. What these businesses need is multiple staff members acting as analysts for their own functional areas and feeding their insights into the collective intelligence of the enterprise. It's therefore become popular to talk about the "democratisation" of data. In a digital business world everyone needs access to customer data and the analytics and visualisation tools used to interpret it and derive actionable insights.

[Data democratisation: this is the possibility for information in a digital format to be accessible to the average end user. The goal of data democratisation is to allow non-specialists to be able to gather and analyse data without requiring outside help.]

A business intelligence strategy connects various information sources and provides staff with easy access to a pool of data, into which they can dive for greater insight. Ultimately, this is the right way forward for all businesses, regardless of scale, because it gives doers direct access to the information they need, sharing the benefits, burden and the accountability for using it to drive performance improvements.

Therefore, the answer to the question of who is responsible for data within an organisation is that every business function should be responsible for its own data. Everyone must have skin in the game. Each business function should be expected to perform their own analysis and act on the insights gleaned. This will align measurement of the success of the strategy very closely with ownership of the strategy implementation. Ideally, there will be an overall co-ordinator within the business, but their job is not to own the data but to orchestrate it, ensuring common data sets, common tools and common standards.

Mine

Once you have defined the data you need, and aligned the business on how you manage, share and act on that information, you then need to ensure that you are extracting the right raw data from your systems to support that.

[Data mining: a process used by companies to turn raw data into useful information.]

Almost every business today has access to "big data". For example, if like millions of other organisations, you use tracking software like Google Analytics, you are capturing a huge volume of data, whether you know it or not. The majority of companies have installed the "out of the box" standard configuration of the software because that's the easiest way to tick the analytics box. But these standard installations were not designed to specifically suit the exact needs of your organisation.

A system may provide access to a huge data set as standard, but it doesn't know what your particular KPIs are. Using the standard configuration of analytics software is limited in value. To reap the full benefit thereof you have to set it up in a way that works for the metrics that are relevant to *your* success. That means activating features that are not automatically enabled when you link the software to your website.

For instance, you will need to set up your "goals". Without tagging those goals you won't know how many visitors are taking the action you need them to take. The ultimate goal may be a sale or enquiry, but you will also have other goals, such as capturing leads, measured by sign-ups for your emails or downloads of content. Otherwise your sales pipeline is going to run dry. If you sell online you will also need to configure your ecommerce tracking so that you can track sales volume and values, as well as the source of those transactions.

You might also want to set up "site search" tracking so that you can identify any gaps between what you visitors are searching for and what you are offering. It's also very useful to set up "segments", so that you can build up a picture of how specific subsets of your visitors are using the website. These could be "first-time visitors" or those from a particular location or almost anything else. You will also want to know which keywords generate the most business. For that you will need to configure "SEO Reports" within Google Analytics. I could go on, but no doubt you get the idea – it's all about the set-up.

Refine

[Refine: to improve something or to make it pure, especially by removing material that is not wanted.]

The days of measuring success based simply on sales numbers are long gone for the most competitive companies. Those numbers just show the *what*. The key metrics are often the diagnostic metrics which together can tell you the *why*. When you know why, you can do something to make it better. That's why organisations of every size and type now "do" tracking and collect data.

Unfortunately, however, relatively few do analysis. There is simply too much information and too little time. Many leaders talk about making data-driven decisions, but only a minority have made it central to their culture. It's important to refine data so that it actually drives improvements to the bottom line, as shown in Figure 17.

Over the years I've seen how the intelligent use of data can give businesses a huge competitive advantage. But I've also seen how the sheer volume of available data creates problems of its own. It's easy to become so overwhelmed by tracking and reporting data that the point of it, to glean insights that can help to improve performance, can be lost. It's those well-known phenomena of data overload and analysis paralysis. Just thinking about the multiple sources of interrelated data variables confronting the modern organisation is enough to bring on a migraine. Here are some of them:

- *Multiple platforms*: back office, finance, CRM and sales systems, website CMS, apps and many more if you have a complex supply chain.
- *Multiple consumer devices*: laptops, desktops, tablets, smartphones.
- *Multiple marketing channels*: online and offline; search, display ads, social and more.
- *Multiple sale channels*: online, call centres, stores.
- *Multiple tracking systems*: different systems being used for tracking websites, sales, social media and more.
- *Multiple target audiences*: segmenting audiences adds another layer of complexity – and opportunity.
- *Multiple customer interactions*: email sign-up, purchase, review, repurchase, browsing, cart abandonments, and so on.

It's important to avoid being swept up by the big data hype. Not all companies should be investing big bucks into collecting and analysing all the available data, at least not immediately. Flooding the team with data, without the resources to use it effectively, is a sure-fire way to waste resources and create confusion. It's way too easy to adopt a "let's just track everything" approach, without taking the time to separate what's important from what's simply nice to know.

There is a high opportunity cost to doing so; the time your people spend on collecting and managing data versus the important work of actual analysis. The Goldilocks challenge is to get the balance just right. Organisations that track too little suffer from blind spots which lead to poor decision-making. But, equally, too much data can lead to valuable insights getting lost in the noise. It's important to nail the fundamentals before you try to become too sophisticated. That means understanding what you need to track and ensuring that you do it accurately. Without that solid platform to work from, trust in the positive power of data can quickly get lost.

It makes sense to begin with a small set of KPIs and supporting metrics, ensuring you can manage them effectively before taking on too much. Ensure you have the capability, capacity and motivation to act on this critical few before moving onwards and upwards. The reality is that most businesses can take great strides by starting with just a few key metrics, tracked by low-cost technology. So, learn what works for your organisation and iteratively build on it, ensuring that any additional metrics really do add value, rather than simply adding work. Once you have nailed the basics and a data-driven culture begins to become embedded in the business, you can increase the level of sophistication.

Let's take marketing attribution as an example of where you can go with analytics. For many years, marketeers have been restricted, in practical terms, to attributing credit for a sale on a "last click" basis. In other words, credit for a sale is given to the last advert, email or other marketing channel that a customer channel (e.g. email) for a sale.

Today, the smartest organisations now have a clear understanding of their customers' entire journeys, across all channels and devices, which they can then use to optimise their marketing spend. They are no longer simply crediting the last click with a sale. They are attributing credit across *all* the channels that assisted them on that sales journey.

The power of data is increased when you put it all together to obtain a more complete picture. When getting physically fit, much of the value of analytics comes from being able combine data from a variety of training sessions over time. In business, the single, best version of truth is also derived from successfully integrating a variety of data inputs. Once you've filtered out the data noise and captured the data you really need, you then have to process that data to make it usable and actionable.

Remember that our brains are wired to process information visually. That's how we connect intellectually and emotionally. Complicated Excel sheets and poorly designed dashboards make it difficult for ordinary mortals to successfully engage with data. So, the way in which we present data really matters. It's not simply that it helps to get the data story across more effectively. It can also help to uncover patterns that have previously gone unnoticed. It's really about making big data "small" enough in volume and format to make it accessible, informative and easily actionable. If big data is about the machines, small data is about people.

Many of us have learned that our efforts to get physically fit and stay in shape can be significantly boosted by having an app dashboard easily accessible on a smartwatch or phone. It helps us to keep track of our performance and progression as well as alerting us if our heart rate gets too high while we're working out. It's provides real-time information when we need it. It's not much use reading a report that warns you about an impending heart attack if you've already woken up in hospital.

It's the same when you're driving your car; you rely on the dashboard to tell you what you need to know at a glance in real time. The amount of data shown is limited to the data that you really need to drive safely. More would make it harder to find the information you need quickly and create a dangerous distraction. All you really need to see is your speed, your fuel level and perhaps directions from your Sat Nav.

Everything else is a nice to have, except in uncommon situations. That's when your car may flash up warnings; maybe the outside temperature is creating icy conditions; maybe your tyres have deflated or a door isn't properly closed. Or perhaps there is a serious problem with your engine. As the driver, you need to be alerted to the situation. Modern cars provide early warning so that you can respond. It may not be clear what the underlying issues are, so your mechanic will plug in their diagnostic tool to find out precisely what's wrong.

That's what it's like to run a business. As a leader you are busy driving. You don't need to become distracted by too much information. You need clearly defined KPIs. But your team need to know how to identify any underlying issues and opportunities with that deeper set of metrics.

In business, a dashboard helps to keep the business focused on the main things. Well-crafted business intelligence dashboards bring your metrics to life, putting your big picture KPIs into the foreground, while allowing users to easily drill down to the diagnostic metrics in the background.

The old school solution of dumping data from multiple systems into an Excel spreadsheet isn't just a massive waste of time. It creates reports that are confusing, hard to read, difficult to decipher, and often too late to be useful. Too much time can be spent manually preparing reports from different datasets. All that activity eats into the time that should be used to derive insights and take the necessary action.

Because of these complications, business intelligence used to be the privilege of large companies who could afford to maintain teams of IT specialists and data scientists. But in the last decade, as technology has developed rapidly, software has become not only more lightweight and powerful, but also more accessible.

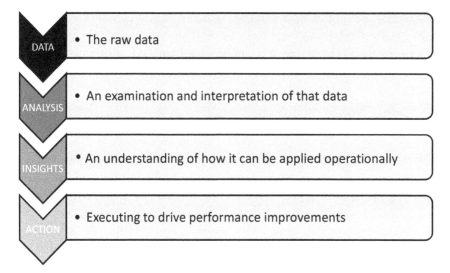

Figure 17 Refining data to make it actionable

Cloud nine

[To be on cloud nine is to be extremely happy and excited.]

New generation, cloud-based technology makes it much easier to turn the raw material into a valuable business asset. If you have ever been on the receiving end of endless requests for reports, or have impatiently awaited their arrival, this will put a big smile on your face, believe me. That's why I've called this section "Cloud nine".

This new and developing technology is a game changer, another key strand in the creation of a digitally fit enterprise, as it helps SMEs to make smarter, data-driven decisions to grow their businesses. Their big data may be relatively small compared to the Amazons of this world, but it can still be complicated. This is usually because of those disparate data sources, such as web analytics, CRM software, selling systems, and more.

Modern business intelligence tools can bring all this data under one roof, allowing analysis to be done in just one place. They integrate data smoothly from multiple sources to help to give a more complete view of performance and early warnings of issues. Think of this software as an interactive dashboard, powered by an integral data warehouse, providing the means for each team member to become their own analyst.

Most web-based tools for smaller businesses follow a self-service model, enabling all members of your team to perform analysis on their own, with no need for the IT department to get involved once it is all set up. Instead of wasting time trying to figure out "who can pull the necessary data," employees can just get on with it.

This new breed of software reminds me of the evolution of website Content Managment Systems. Early websites were pretty static because staff had to go back to the programmers to get anything changed, even a small piece of copy. That had a cost implication in both time and money. Now we have much more sophisticated CMSs, which despite their massively improved functionality, are now easy for any non-technical staff members to use. This has enabled the burden of changing and updating content to be shared across an organisation, reducing costs and avoiding IT bottlenecks.

Business intelligence tools have gone through the same evolution. The new breed of tools is versatile so that it can meet the needs of customers in a wide variety of different industries and functions. Staff in any department can be armed with drag-and-drop business dashboards that help them to be autonomously data-driven without extensive training, programming knowledge or an on-call data scientist. Business intelligence solutions typically include data visualisation software that can quickly create compelling charts without people having to spend hours on chart formatting and design. The best new tools do it for them, so that they can focus on the important stuff – such as actually acting on their insights to improve performance.

Smart business intelligence tools also increase collaboration by providing data access wherever employees are, an increasingly important factor as the popularity of remote working increases. This keeps staff on the same page in that they are empowered to view the same data from multiple locations and make data-driven decisions together.

Another benefit of such systems, as with all cloud applications, is that major upfront investment in hardware isn't required. You pay for the functionalities and capacity you need today, but, thanks to the subscription model, you can scale up and add more features as the need for analytics increases. This approach is a perfect fit for SMEs with big growth potential, where it's critical for the capability of software to flex with the business.

The more you empower individuals to use and share data, the better their access to vital customer, operational and financial information, the more effective they will be in contributing to the achievement of your goals. The key to any pre-built solution is that it must help you to make decisions. Any business intelligence tool that doesn't make it easy to find the answer to your specific business questions is a waste of money.

Information pours into your company every hour, day and night. Don't just store it or ignore it. Harness that data effectively to get ahead of the pack. It's a very real source of competitive advantage, helping smaller businesses to outmanoeuvre the bigger fish. Those bigger fish may be better funded and have more data experts, but while they go through multiple layers of approvals to get any change through, you can get busy acting on the insights.

To get to the why – the actual insights – you will often need to combine data, and do some slicing and dicing, to use another technical term. Only then will you get to the heart of the story that the data is trying to tell. And it is a story. Data doesn't have to be dull. Dull doesn't inspire us to get stuff done.

Digitally fit businesses don't do dull or sit around guessing. They test. They track. They prove and demonstrate with data. They are able to easily access that data and make sense of it to see what's really happening in the business. Once again, the defining characteristic of these organisations is that they harness technology effectively in order to enhance the power – in this case the decision-making power – of their people.

Let's round off the data component section by summarising some of the ways in which data can help organisations, keeping in mind the words of Andrew Lang: "I shall try not to use statistics as a drunken man uses lampposts, for support rather than for illumination".

1   The source of truth

Sometimes the truth hurts. But at least raw data gives you it to you straight – at least if you're tracking correctly. If you are, it should be impossible to manipulate data to tell you what you want to hear. It may tell you that you've only had ten people visit your website since the start of the week and that they all left within three seconds of landing. Or that 90 per cent of your visitors in the past month were returning users and therefore your site is failing to attracting new prospects. This information is precious. It tells you what is really going on in your business.

2   Waste management

At the heart of digital business, particularly in sales and marketing, is the ability to track performance accurately and to enable decisions to be taken quickly in order to maximise opportunities and cut waste. Data can also help to reduce risk; new products, marketing and processes can be closely monitored to quickly show performance trends before investment is ramped up.

3   The secret to improved performance:

Because data tells you the truth, it can establish a baseline from which to measure improvement. It is only by quantifying something that you can objectively track the incremental impact of decisions. A series of micro-targets is the name of the game, focusing on doing things that will drive improvements one day at a time. Ultimately, data is the best defence against HiPPO decision-making. As Jim Barksdale, former Netscape CEO put it: "If we have data, let's look at data. If all we have are opinions, let's go with mine".

4   Control, collaboration and autonomy

Digital business data provides businesses of all sizes with the opportunity to work smarter, maximising their use of resources. This helps leaders to track performance and progress and helps doers to demonstrate value, ROI and highlight issues that require decisions from the top. It frees up the organisation's frontline staff to execute while leaders can maintain control, secure in the knowledge that the budget is being *visibly* invested in areas giving the greatest return. Therefore, data can encourage teamwork by identifying focus areas and making performance more transparent. When all of a company's functions are working together towards a common goal, they can make data insights meaningful and valuable, while simultaneously increasing team motivation and involvement levels.

5   A crystal ball (almost)

Because data gives you an objective view, it can be used to help to predict the future. Of course, just because something happened today doesn't mean it will happen tomorrow, but it can reveal trends and patterns that give you a much clearer perspective. For example, if your analytics data is telling you that mobile traffic to your site is growing every month, you can reasonably predict that it will continue to grow and that you should therefore invest in a responsive website design. Or, if your data is telling you that customers who buy a particular set of products typically stay with you for three years, you can calculate lifetime value to inform when and how much you should pay to acquire them. Data will never tell you exactly what the future holds, but it can be a very good guide to what is likely to happen.

6   Your competitive edge

Your data, be that marketing performance or customer data from your CRM, is unique to your business. It is your biggest asset. Your competitors can't see it. Only you have the means to fully understand how your customers research and buy. Data also helps leaders to check out the competition; by using publicly available, low-cost web tools they can uncover how competitors are getting results. It will also help them to identify gaps in the market, revealing new opportunities. They can then move on from guesswork and gut decision-making to action, based on firm evidence.

7   A means to build relationships

It's the little things that make a difference in a relationship. It's no use talking about customer focus if you don't really listen to your customers and get a deep understanding of what makes them tick. That's what data is all about – identifying patterns of customer behaviour so that you can get closer to them. Insights about what makes them buy, how they prefer to shop, why they switch, what they'll buy next, and what factors lead them to recommend a company to others can help you to make better business decisions. Data can also help to build better supplier relationships by enabling faster analysis of supplier performance and working with them to anticipate customer demand patterns.

8   A troubleshooting short cut

To get the root of problems so that you can solve them quickly.

9   A more convincing way to tell your story

To investors, board members and other stakeholders. It's all about the numbers for these audiences.

10 A big, competitive weapon for businesses of any size

It's not just the big organisations such as banks that benefit from this big data. Even the smallest companies can use the new breed of affordable digital technology to get insights from their data that give them a real competitive edge.

Ultimately, taking control of data isn't about letting the machines make decisions for us. It's about using them to collate and present information in an easy to understand way, helping us to make sense of it so that we can make better business choices. Figure 18 provides a summary of the issues and action that can be taken to make better use of performance data.

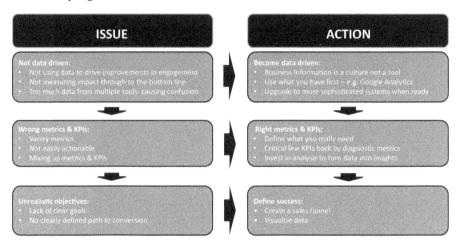

Figure 18 Issues and actions for a better use of data

Confine

Data is the new business currency and like other currencies you need to keep it safe from those who covet it. They could be competitors, hackers or staff who are thinking of going it alone. Most of all you also have an obligation to keep it safe for those who entrusted you with it in the first place – your prospects and customers.

The penalties for failing to keep data safe and manage it responsibly can be severe. It's not just the reputational damage any more. Consumers have become much savvier about how their data is being used and traded and they are demanding higher standards of use, greater security and more control over their privacy. Increasingly, legislators around the world are answering those calls through stricter regulations and punitive fines. A good example is the European Union GDPR initiative.

The threat of data theft is very real of course, as global hackers seek out security weaknesses in vulnerable enterprises. Data security and privacy have to be important considerations for all business leaders in the twenty-first century. Leaders should not forget that all information has a value. Small or large, all businesses retain sensitive data within systems from financial records to their CRM. The golden rule is that if it's important to you, it's likely to be important to criminal hackers too.

While it's true to say that some smaller businesses have stayed under the radar for data theft, leaders of SMEs should not believe that cyber criminals will continue to ignore them. As larger organisations invest in stronger digital security defences, the bad guys are increasingly turning their attention towards the smaller firms. As with many digital technologies the barriers to acquiring tools have lessened considerably. Attack tools are now readily available to buy or rent from the Dark Web, complete with online support services at low cost.

In the United States, research by the Federation of Small Businesses shows that two thirds of SMBs were the victims of cybercrime between 2014–2016. So, those that haven't been affected are now in the minority and attack figures are climbing fast. It's not generally a question of budget. Cyber security doesn't necessarily mean investing in expensive software. The weakest link in the security chain is often humans, so the right employee habits, protocols and technical controls can mitigate much of the risk. But there are several other important do's and don'ts:

- Do ensure that software updates and patches can run, preferably set to automatic. Attacks often target these vulnerabilities to infect computers and networks worldwide.

- Do avoid using out-of-date systems, such as old versions of MS Windows. Some of these versions are no longer supported or updated by Microsoft and are therefore at particular risk.

- Do familiarize yourself with the IASME standard, recognized by the UK government as the most comprehensive cyber security standard. IASME is an Information Assurance standard that is designed to be simple and affordable to help to improve the cyber security of SMEs. It details eleven steps that businesses can take to minimise risk, of which seven cost almost nothing. There are no doubt similar standards in the United States and many other countries.

- Don't use lack of expertise as an excuse for inaction. There are a number of free resources available from the National Cyber Security Centre – both for individuals and organisations of various scales. Increasing education and awareness has been proven to reduce risk. Businesses can also undertake "Cyber Essentials" as part of IASME, to provide assurance to customers and demonstrate their commitment to cyber security.

- Do consider outsourcing to help your business to fill gaps where internal knowledge falls short. But make sure you are working with a trusted supplier. Ultimately, your business will still own the risk and the impact of any attack.

- Do familiarise yourselves with all present and planned regulations. Again, in Europe you need to understand the implications of the GDPR, which has had a big impact on how businesses do data-driven marketing. It gives consumers new levels of protection and control over their data. Organisations have new legal responsibilities in the way they handle data, be it information about prospects, employees or customer records.

Many business intelligence tools provide data warehousing solutions which involve moving all or part of business data to a secure data storage facility. Although the idea of moving sensitive corporate data to a cloud-based data warehouse may worry leaders, it can in fact significantly reduce security concerns. Implementing the cloud means that your data is put into the care of specialists, who have to comply with strict security standards and are subject to regular security audits. There are also the practical benefits of cloud-based data warehousing, such as less concern about lost laptops, laden with confidential data. It also simplifies the process of data back-up and recovery, and that translates into reduced costs.

If data is to remain an important currency in the years to come, businesses must not only keep their customer data safe, they must also be responsible and sensitive in the way they use it. Retailers have been using predictive analytics for years to help to understand customer buying patterns. Companies are tracking and combining consumers' browsing and purchase history, using point of sale, marketing, web data, social media and loyalty data to make informed decisions about pricing, promotions, demand forecasting and price optimisation.

Such data can be used to predict what customers may want to buy next, providing incremental value to them by giving them visibility of offers and products that they otherwise might miss. But sometimes it can be tempting to overstep the mark. For example, it is possible that a retailer could know that a woman is pregnant before her loved ones do if she decides to wait until she's sure before she breaks the news. The merchant simply needs to match the pages viewed and advertisements clicked to that individual, using a unique identifier of some kind. If the content consistently relates to babies, then a retailer can draw a conclusion about the type of products she may be receptive to and start making recommendations that may be seen by others.

That's an extreme but very real example, and the privacy ethics are questionable to say the least. It could also be commercially damaging. It is easy to imagine somebody going off a brand pretty quickly, perhaps demanding that all their data be removed from that company's databases if they become too intrusive. Just because something is technically possible doesn't mean it's the right thing to do.

Again, some human qualities of empathy and sensitivity are required in the mix to ensure that the opportunities to add real value don't cross the lines of acceptability or common courtesy. People must remain in control, not the technology. There is a significant value to people in providing data as customers, as well as a clear value to the organisations they allow to use it. But that contract is based on trust which takes considerably longer to earn than it does to lose.

Need-to-know workout tips: ten steps to becoming
a data-driven organisation

1   Getting started

- Developing a data-driven culture will take time – it's a process.
- The best approach is to start with simple innovations and allow these to evolve so that the organisation can adjust without suffering from data overload and analysis paralysis.

2   Assess and define

- Where are we now? Do a data audit. What tracking is in place? How is it configured?
- Identify any barriers: is there the capacity and capability to undertake analysis and deliver insights?
- What are the requirements from all stakeholders? What questions do they want answers to on a regular basis?
- Who owns and has responsibility for management, analysis/interpretation, communicating and actions. Is that a bottleneck?

3   KPIs/metrics

- Concentrate on the "critical few" KPIs – too many will dilute focus.
- Take a layered approach; ensure that top-level data is supported in a logical way by metrics that provide the detailed diagnostics and insights.

4   Share and act

- Create an intelligent, digitally fit business, with actionable insights, shared across the team.
- Use cloud-based business intelligence software when you are ready to step up.

5   Make it easy to understand and relevant.

- The aesthetics can make a big difference in helping the audience to see the data story.

- Ensure that the right data is presented succinctly to the right internal audiences. Don't make people wade through data that is irrelevant to their specific needs.
- Look at data using a variety of chart types to see it from different angles.

6 Focus on trends

- The best insights often come from looking at trends rather than singular data points, especially when the trends change direction.

7 Compare time ranges

- Look at data across different time ranges, such as week over week, month over month or year on year, as well against the goals that you have set.

8 Look for relationships

- Often, the most powerful insights come from an analysis of the relationships between two or more variables.

9 Seek different perspectives

- We all see things differently. Get the input of others to reveal insights that may have been missed.

10 Challenge

- Ensure that the data is robust by checking how that data is tracked and that you are always comparing like for like.

- Data can mislead as well as inform, so make sure it's telling the story accurately.

Component 6: Agility

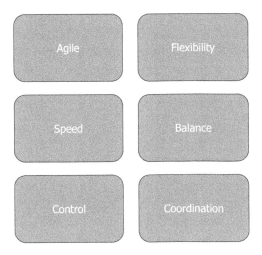

Figure 19 Agility six-pack

Agile

[Agile: this relates to or denotes a method of project management, used especially for software development, that is characterised by the division of tasks into short phases of work and the frequent reassessment and adaptation of plans.]

Making a shift to Agile is not easy, particularly for organisations with very hierarchal structures and entrenched silos. To begin with, an enterprise's primary mission must shift from a goal of simply making money to a goal of delighting the customer. This is a fundamental point and can be difficult be for leaders to embrace. Most leaders have become conditioned to think about revenue, margin and profit first, rather than thinking about customer value and satisfaction as a means to achieve those very important financial outcomes.

Agile techniques originated in the software development community as an alternative to the classic planning approach to business management, which proved increasingly unfit for purpose in a digital business world. As a set of methodologies, it is by no means perfect. But, as a set of principles, it fits a digital business mindset with a customer-centric and continual optimisation ethos. It doesn't guarantee success. But with a focus on delivering work in small chunks, we will find out quickly if we are right or wrong.

[Business agility: this refers to the distinct qualities that allow organisations to respond rapidly to changes in the internal and external environment without losing momentum or vision. Adaptability, flexibility and balance are three qualities that are essential to long-term business agility.]

I think of agility more as a business philosophy than a methodology. It is essentially a set of values and principles, a way of interacting and thinking differently about how we do our work. The objective is, of course, to achieve better outcomes with less effort. It's as much about changing the attitudes and behaviours of a team, as it is about leadership style. *Doing* Agile (capital "A") with a methodology or formal Agile process gets limited results compared to actually *being* agile (small "a") and changing the business, team and people at its core.

When an agile approach becomes part of an organisation's culture, teams begin to readily accept and expect change. They begin to think about how they can take advantage of it and reduce the impact of ambiguity, uncertainty and complexity.

In practice it comprises several ideas:

- *Responsiveness*: reacting more quickly to changing circumstances and opportunities.
- *Sprints*: consistently delivering smaller increments of value, rather than big projects that can take months or years to deliver any value.
- *Testing*: experimenting to learn and improve performance.
- *Analytics*: measuring performance to show whether the changes have made a positive impact.
- *Customer*: as the boss. It is *their* reaction and feedback to your enhancements that really counts.
- *Reprioritising*: work constantly to make sure that the most important things are being worked on.

Speed

There's no doubt that business today moves faster. In order to succeed we all have to make decisions faster, identify opportunities faster and get our products to market faster. The only way to keep up is to create a culture of agility. All the other five focus areas we have looked at so far – mindset, core strength, skills, power and data – contribute to an agile ethos characterised by flexibility, adaptability, balance and co-ordination.

It doesn't mean that "we'll just make it up as we go along". It's not about endless analysis and debate. It is about making decisions quickly and acting decisively. In other words, less pontificating and more doing. Earlier, I wrote about the concept of Design Thinking, which is central to an agile way of working. Essentially, it's a way to improve productivity by achieving "clarity through action". It's about getting work done efficiently in order to implement the strategy and react to changing market conditions. It is no use developing your core strengths if you don't have agility. Power without agility is really just mass.

As with data, the key to business agility is transparency. Leaders need teams to be transparent in terms of communicating their progress. The teams themselves also need time to reflect and test before getting into the next sprint.

Leaders of digitally fit enterprises empower their people to make innovation, specifically customer-driven innovation, a business as usual activity. They know they have succeeded when their people stop thinking about improvements as a project, but treat it as an everyday focus, through a combination of culture, mission, muscle memory and a simple desire to make things better. You may also notice that your best employees stop leaving.

So, for example, let's assume that the website doers in your team have looked at the analytics, received feedback from customers and picked up on a slew of comments on social media about an issue on your website. Do they then start a motivation-sapping process to make the case for the changes, seek approval and then schedule the work? Or do they just get on and fix it, providing leaders with before and after data to show that the effort was worthwhile?

I know as a leader which option I prefer. I've seen organisations that take months to fix simple issues on a website that could and should have been done within hours. This is often, but not always, the result of an ostensibly agile web team being held back by an old school IT hierarchy that is as agile as a sedated snail. Yes, there will be issues that need to go upstairs for a decision or bigger issues that need a business case. But where there is an obvious bug fix or enhancement, it needs to be sorted out as quickly as possible, not simply put on a growing "to do" list.

Often, I've seen those lists grow so long that a committee is formed to make a call on which items should receive priority development status. Such committees are frequently made up of people who aren't very close to the customer. The committee decision-making process is often further complicated by the need of those people to seek explanations of each proposed change, because they are not intimately involved, thereby creating further development tailbacks.

Having said that, in the real world, resources can't always keep up with demand. So, there will need to be a process for deciding what to do in what order, when every change request gets pitched as a priority, as people try and jump the queue. The key is to let the agile team decide themselves. I always encourage teams to score the urgency required based on a quick calculation of the customer impact of each issue. Again, the data should inform these decisions.

Of course, agility isn't simply about having the information and authority to make decisions. It's also about having the wherewithal to act on those decisions. That means you need to ask yourself as a leader whether you have the resources, skills, organisational structure, technical infrastructure and tools to make agility a reality rather than an aspiration.

For example, does your website CMS enable changes to be made by non-technical staff without getting the coders involved at all? Does it have the functionality to help you to manage the governance of this freedom to act? The trick is to have the right people, processes and technical platforms working together, so that meetings can be restricted to short daily stand-up meetings, leaving most of the hours in the day free to actually get the good stuff done.

Control

Agile changes the role of leaders. At the heart of the agile culture is trust. Leaders of digitally fit enterprises trust those who are closer to the customer to prioritise work effectively and work out the best way to do it. They recognise that in their role as coach they cannot be on the pitch with their team. This is a vital element of digital fitness: replacing a one-way, top-down chain of command and control with more horizontal conversations is key to speeding up decision-making.

This contrasts with traditional hierarchies in which bosses identify what needs to be done and then instruct their underlings to do it. Within hierarchies, employees have to trust the wisdom of their leaders. But within an agile culture, this notion gets turned on its head: leaders empower their employees. Decision-making authority is pushed down to the doers.

Co-ordination and collaboration are central to an agile way of doing the work. As with decision-making, instead of those doing the work reporting as individuals to the boss, the work is done in self-organising teams. The bottom line is that a business simply cannot be fast and agile if people have to keep running to the senior management team every time a decision has to be made.

The predominant values must be transparency and continuous improvement, driven by teamwork and a laser-like customer focus. It can be a tough concept for leaders to adapt to, because in some important ways they need to defer to the customer as the boss. It seems like a loss of power, because it flips the traditional managerial modus operandi. But leaders can console themselves with the thought that it's much more empowering and rewarding to lead successful agile teams, than it is to manage constricted failing teams.

Data, and the insights derived from it, become the main driver, helping leaders to quickly understand what's happening in the business and the wider market it operates in. If they are smart about the way insights are shared across the organisation, they can empower their people to take good data-driven decisions. This may seem somewhat utopian to some, but I have seen the difference it can make to levels of motivation and successful implementations. It is particularly important in a digital world for two reasons.

Firstly, it's because digital speeds up implementation. New ideas and approaches can be tested very quickly and at a comparatively low cost compared to analogue, where physical things need to be designed and produced. Importantly, updates and enhancements can usually be rolled back if there's an unexpected problem or the execution doesn't deliver the expected result.

Secondly, in a period where many businesses are led by digital immigrants, but much of the workforce are digital natives, fault lines can develop, causing a rift between directors and doers that drastically slows progress. If an organisation cannot adapt to this new way of thinking, departing from a fundamental belief in the effectiveness of the top-down "the leader is the boss" approach, it's difficult to implement agile ways of working effectively. There will always be ongoing friction between the different goals and approaches, resulting in little if any improvement in the company. The name of the game in modern organisations today is persuading managers to stop acting like a boss, embrace agility and become customer obsessed.

It's a fundamental part of developing as a leader when you understand that it's more important to coach than to control and command. Leadership today must be more about conditioning minds and training individuals to think and work as a team, while at the same time, making sure that each individual makes their contribution with intensity and skill.

This same tension between intuitive and analytical styles can be seen in many organisations. In my experience, business leaders, like coaches, are often in one camp or another. Some prefer an evidence-driven approach supported by data and analysis, while others prefer a more instinctive approach based on experience and gut feeling. Leaders of digitally fit organisations understand that these should not be seen as opposing philosophies but rather as complementary types of intelligence. Together they help us to see the whole picture and enable us to take the right decisions at the right time.

Agility doesn't mean that you need to simply throw away the old playbook and say goodbye to proper business disciplines such as governance, budgeting, and planning. But it does mean that governance and planning is based on outcomes and the value created, quantified by hard data, rather than documents and box ticking. After all, action speaks louder than words.

In practice, most organisations are not culturally equipped to quickly adopt full-blown Agile (capital "A") management techniques, and therefore, at least in the short term, they typically take a hybrid approach. Effectively, this is based on increasing levels of autonomy and collaboration, within a more defined implementation roadmap. But creating an increasingly agile culture should be the ambition of all leaders who aspire to run a digitally fit organisation.

Flexibility

Leaders of digitally fit organisations should also build flexibility into their budgeting and other processes to enable faster reactions to changes in their business environments. None of us can see into the future with absolute clarity but we can prepare our organisations to pivot quickly when opportunities and threats emerge.

Many transformation efforts are hampered by budgetary cycles that are insufficiently responsive to business requirements in flight. It's not enough to just periodically check spend against revenue at the macro level. In a digital business world, we must continually measure performance against a series of micro ambitions and make constant adjustments to optimise performance.

Let's take marketing as our example again. Traditionally, marketing budgets were set for the year, usually based on a percentage of turnover. That budget was like a block of ice, solid but melting away throughout the year as the money was spent on a series of pre-planned campaigns. Today, in the always-on digital world, a marketing budget must be fluid. Instead of a block of ice, think of it more as a controlled stream of water directed by a flexible tap.

The frontline marketing team must be allowed to control the direction and flow of budget, based on constant tracking and testing of tactics. When you are tracking the ROI of your marketing channels, measuring how they are performing individually and collectively, you can, and should, be refining your tactics constantly, based on the results you are getting.

The idea of spending a fixed amount on marketing in a particular digital channel and then stopping, even if the data shows you are making a positive return on investment, is ridiculous. It's true that you may get decreasing ROI the more you use a channel or tactic. Returns tend not to be linear.

But as long as it's generating an adequate return, why stop unless you have supply issues? It doesn't make any sense, but I've seen it happen frequently because of the way budgets are run.

Again, it doesn't mean relinquishing all control: the governance is robust tracking that everybody trusts. The management control is that easy access to data that shows performance. Remember that old school marketing was largely based on campaigns. It operated on a command-and-control process with heavy planning up front, deadlines tied to product releases, and retrospective measurement to see if all that creativity and hard work actually delivered. Any software developers would recognize this as the "waterfall" development process that they have now dumped in favour of Agile methods – or at least hybrid agile approaches.

Balance

Agile also means having the mindset and means to test small before you go big on a new product or proposition. Jim Collins famously talked about the need to "Shoot bullets before cannon balls". Of course, he meant that leaders should take small steps before committing to giant leaps and big solutions. It's really just another way of saying that if you are going to fail when innovating, make sure you do it fast and at relatively low cost. It's about getting the balance between innovation and investment right.

Digital is made for firing bullets. Research, testing, publishing, promotion and evaluation is all much easier in a digital space. Bullets are cheaper to make and easier to fire than cannonballs. Wise leaders repetitively test ideas and assumptions in low-risk, low-cost ways. They ask: what worked? What didn't? What cost too much, even if it worked? Then, after testing, evaluation and adaptation, they wheel out the heavy artillery to build on their small-scale successes.

Co-ordination

All organisations need to make silos disappear, except those that store grain or guided missiles. And so co-ordination is the sixth element within the Agility digital fitness component.

[Silo mentality: this attitude is found in some organisations, and occurs when several departments or groups within an organisation do not want to share information or knowledge with other individuals in the wider team. A silo mentality reduces the organisation's efficiency and can contribute to a failing corporate culture.]

In my experience, it's not always a question of attitude. Typically, a silo mentality is simply a result of the realities of separation and its negative effect on cross-communication within an organisation. With the exception of micro-businesses, every company has some compartmentalised business functions such as marketing, sales, finance, production, IT, fulfilment and customer service. In larger organisations there will also be silos *within* silos. For example, the marketing function may contain brand, internal communications, advertising and digital silos. A sales function may be split by channel, such as retail stores, online and customer contact centres, often set up as separate business units competing with each other for business.

Silos are probably the biggest single barrier to the creation of an agile, customer-focused organisation. The problem with silos is that they are brilliant at inhibiting the flow of information and collaboration. And that gets in the way of cross-functional teamwork. But silos are not only caused by organisational structures. They can also be created by the variety of tools being used within the business. Technology can create walls as well.

Simply trying to smash down the walls between functions can be counterproductive. Nobody likes to see the bulldozers move in and a healthy culture of collaboration does not tend to thrive on resentment. Instead, the focus must be on making the silos disappear. That means that rather than bullying everybody into working more closely together, leaders use their unifying vision and culture, supported by technology, as their silo solvents.

There are a number of practical steps you can take. One that has worked well for me is the use of cloud project management and collaboration systems. You may well use them already. These systems are practical in the way they facilitate the sharing and management of information. But their real value is that they remove the veil that can cover each person's contribution to a project or programme of change. That helps to show everyone how much work is being done by other functions within projects as well as highlighting accountability. Again, everything becomes transparent and there are no hiding places.

In my experience people in one business function often have a limited understanding of the contribution of other functions within the organisation. They don't really know the ins and outs of what others do, so tend to assume it's not very much. Making the workings visible tends to mitigate that. A good dollop of mutual respect and understanding is a good foundation for effective collaboration. Another useful habit is holding regular inter-departmental show and tells, where representatives of each function can talk through the things they are doing to improve customer experience.

Not all functions are set up to move at the same speed. This can create frustrations if one function feels that it is being slowed down by dependence on another function that operates at a slower cadence. For example, if the IT function runs a release cycle of six weeks, the person in marketing who is trying to get rapid customer feedback on a new website feature is going to have to wait. If that happens repeatedly, it puts an organisation at a competitive disadvantage. Leaders must work to understand these productivity blockers, balancing motivations, comfort and urgency to foster better performance.

As Sam Altman put it: "You can create value with breakthrough innovation, incremental refinement, or complex coordination. Great companies often do two of these. The very best companies do all three".

I also like this quote from Will Durant: "We are what we repeatedly do, excellence then is not an act, but a habit".

[Muscle memory: the ability to reproduce a particular movement without conscious thought, acquired as a result of frequent repetition of that movement.]

When you get your organisation in great shape for a digital future you will have achieved a kind of organisational muscle memory, whereby new ways of working, enabled by digital technologies, become second nature. Think of it as an organisational cache, storing the ability to perform complex actions unconsciously without the constant drag of having to tap into the conscious mind. These procedures and processes must be learnt and then embedded through repetition. Like physical fitness it's about building habits, creating those new pathways in our brain that help us to do things correctly and automatically as part of our normal routine.

Need-to-know workout tips: what does an agile bionic business look like?

1 Speed

- Fast reaction times.
- Quicker decisions and implementations when presented with strategic opportunities and market shifts.
- By empowering people within their teams in a cultural context of trust, innovation and risk-taking.
- Smart use of technology teamed with streamlined processes within a flattened hierarchy.

2   *Customer-focused above all else*

- Intimate understanding of customers' needs and behaviour to anticipate their future requirements so that they can act quickly and proactively rather than reactively.

3   *Co-ordination*

- A "team before self" attitude.
- The recognition that although individual stars will always be important, being digitally fit requires a collaborative team effort across the entire customer journey to purchase.

4   *Adaptability*

- A growth mindset at the heart of their culture.
- At both the individual and organisational level, from the boardroom to the front line.

Bibliography

Auster, Ellen R., Wylie, K. and Valente, M. (2005) *Strategic Organizational Change*. Basingstoke: Palgrave Macmillan.

Bendle, N., Farris, P., Pfeifer, P. and Reibstein, D. (2016) *Marketing Metrics*. Upper Saddle River, NJ: Pearson Education.

Blanchard, K. and Johnson, S. (2012) *The One Minute Manager*. London: HarperCollins.

Brown, Tim (2008) Design Thinking. Available at https://hbr.org/2008/06/designthinking (accessed 11 February 2018).

Chaffey D. (2017) Introducing RACE: A Practical Framework to Improve Your Digital Marketing. Available at www.smartinsights.com/digital-marketing-strategy/race-a-practicalframework-to-improve-your-digital-marketing (accessed 4 March 2018).

Collins, J. and Hansen, M. (2011) *Great by Choice*. New York: HarperCollins.

Collins, J. and Porras, J. (2005) *Built to Last*. London: Random House Business Books.

Darwin, C. (1872) *The Expression of the Emotions in Man and Animals*. London: John Murray.

Dweck, C. (2015) *Mindset*. Clitheroe: Joosr.

entrepreneur.com (2017) Trigger These 4 Key Brain Chemicals for Happier Workers. Available at www.entrepreneur.com/article/287903 (accessed 26 March 2018).

Evans, Martin and Scott, Patrick (2017) Fraud and Cyber-Crime Are Now the Country's Most Common Offences. *The Telegraph*. Available at www.telegraph.co.uk/news/2017/01/19/fraud-cyber-crimenow-countrys-common-offences/ (accessed 12 March 2018).

Forbes.com (2018) Charles Koch. Available at www.forbes.com/100-greatest-business-minds/person/charles-koch (accessed 13 April 2018).

Frei, Frances and Morriss, Anne (2012) Culture Takes Over When the CEO Leaves the Room. *Harvard Business Review*. Available at https://hbr.org/2012/05/culture-takes-over-when-the-ce (accessed 13 November 2017).

Fripp, Patricia (2016) 10 Sell Yourself Strategies for Speakers. Available at www.fripp.com/10-sell-yourself-strategies-for-speakers/ (accessed 29 March 2018).

fsb.org.uk (2016) Cyber Resilience: How to Protect Small Firms in the Digital Economy. Available at www.fsb.org.uk/docs/default-source/fsb-org-uk/fsb-cyberresilience-report-2016.pdf (accessed 19 March 2018).

Gallo, A. (2014) The Value of Keeping the Right Customers. *Harvard Business Review*. Available at https://hbr.org/2014/10/the-value-of-keeping-the-right-customers (accessed 13 April 2018).

Hill, Emily (2016) What Is 'Being in the Zone'? The Fascinating Psychology of Super Productivity (June). Available at www.huffingtonpost.com/emily-hill/what-it-really-means-to-b_b_10300610.html (accessed 14 April 2018).

Horton, H. (2018). No More Working 9 to 5? Vast Majority of Britons Now Work Different Hours, Study Shows. *The Telegraph*. Available at www.telegraph.co.uk/news/2018/08/21/no-working-9-5-vast-majority-britons-now-work-different-hours/ (accessed 13 September 2018).

Huntress, Caelan. (2017) My Favourite Quote of All Time Is a Misattribution (24 August). Available at https://caelanhuntress.com/2017/08/24/my-favourite-quote-of-all-time-is-a-misattribution/ (accessed 20 March 2018).

IASME (n.d.) Available at https://en.wikipedia.org/wiki/IASME (accessed 11 March 2018).

Jones, Bruce (2014) Leadership Lessons from Walt Disney: Perfecting the Customer Experience. Available at https://disneyinstitute.com/blog/2014/09/leadership-lessons-from-waltdisney-perfecting-the-customer-experience/ (accessed 23 January 2018).

Mattin, David (2017) Your Internal Culture Is Your Brand. Available at https://shift.newco.co/in-2017-you-internal-culture-is-your-brand-cdbfef131cff (accessed 20 December 2017).

Payton, Susan (2014) The Zig Ziglar School of Sales: How to Overcome 5 Basic Sales Obstacles. Available at https://blog.getbase.com/the-zig-ziglar-school-of-sales-how-to-overcome5-basic-sales-obstacles (accessed 12 March 2018).

Pullizi, J. (2015) *Content Inc: How Entrepreneurs Use Content to Build Massive Audiences and Create Radically Successful Businesses*. New York: McGraw-Hill Education.

Rouse, Margaret (2015) Data Democratization. Available at http://whatis.techtarget.com/definition/data-democratization (accessed 11 February 2018).

Senge, Peter (1990) *The Fifth Discipline: The Art and Practice of the Learning Organization.* London: Century Business.

Shukairy, A. (n.d.). Usability 101: Designing for a Better User Experience. Available at www.invespcro.com/blog/usability-101-designing-for-a-better-user-experience/ (accessed 5 May 2018).

Silver, Nate (2012) Nate Silver Explains How His Model Trounced Polling Establishment on Election Day. Available at www.inquisitr.com/394303/natesilver-explains-how-his-model-trounced-polling-establishment-on-election-day/ (accessed 17 December 2017).

Statista.com (2018) Number of Smartphone Users Worldwide from 2014 to 2020 (in billions). Available at www.statista.com/statistics/330695/number-of-smartphone-users-worldwide/ (accessed 13 September 2018).

Stephens-Davidowitz, S. (2017) *Everybody Lies*. London: Bloomsbury.

Stern, Stefan (2011) The Importance of Creating and Keeping a Customer (10 October). Available at www.ft.com/content/88803a36-f108-11e0-b56f-00144feab49a (accessed 26 January 2018).

The Future of Jobs (n.d.). The Future of Jobs. Available at http://reports.weforum.org/future-of-jobs-2016/?doing_wp_cron=1536070952.6344089508056640625000   The Future of Jobs (accessed 16 April 2018).

Welch, J. and Welch, S. (2014) *Winning*. HarperCollins e-Books.

Part 4

Get with the programme

Time to get in shape – the complete get fit for digital business programme

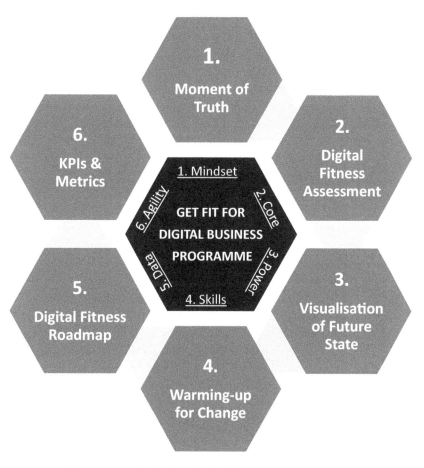

Figure 20 Get fit for digital business programme

[A digitally fit business: a collaborative, connected, flexible and future-ready organisation, where skilled and agile cross-functional teams work in harmony with digital technology to develop customer experience superpowers.]

The digital world really took off in 1990 when computer scientist Tim Berners-Lee invented the World Wide Web. In the intervening thirty years, digital adaptation has been enough to keep many businesses in the game. But that phase is coming to an end.

We've seen it before in business, working to a similar timescale, with another game changer – electricity. Thomas Edison built his first generating stations in London and New York in the early 1880s. There were some early adopters, but it took another forty years or so for electricity to supplant steam as the most prevalent power source in manufacturing and to become fully integrated into peoples' personal and working lives.

There were good reasons for this. It took time for the infrastructure to develop and costs to reduce, of course. But perhaps the biggest reason was that it takes time for businesses to work out how to fully harness new technology and apply fundamentally new operating models across their entire value chain. When businesses fully evolved in the early twentieth century, electricity produced some dramatic increases in productivity. Not only that, but it greatly improved working conditions, and therefore the well-being of employees. Gone was the heat and pollution generated by gas lighting, along with the significant fire hazard.

Digital is like electricity. It didn't take long for organisations to connect to it. But it will only begin to deliver significant gains in productivity and what we could call organisational well-being, when the majority of businesses have moved on from adaptation – where digital is deployed tactically as a way of doing the same old things in a faster, cheaper way – to evolution, where digital is used to fundamentally change the way business is actually done.

Getting fit for digital business is a process. It takes time and as a result can't be left on the back burner any longer. "Those who think they have not time for bodily exercise will sooner or later have to find time for illness". Edward Stanley's words should resonate in the minds of SME business leaders today. If they are serious about growth, productivity and ultimately long-term survival they must become proactive. Otherwise, like an out of shape human body, their enterprise is likely to face health challenges down the track.

Like a jigsaw puzzle, digital transformation doesn't make much sense when the pieces are tipped out of the box and scattered over the table. It's only when leaders have a framework that progress really begins. After all, puzzles are best solved frame first, working towards the centre, because it helps to make the process of finding the right combination of pieces much easier.

The get fit for digital business framework supports a balanced, holistic and human approach to change, designed not only to improve business performance in a digital world, but also to improve the overall well-being of an organisation. Of course, it is not an "out of the box" answer to everything.

There can never be a one size fits all digital transformation recipe. Organisations come in too many shapes and sizes for that. Each will have unique requirements, challenges and opportunities, depending on scale, location and whether they are B2B or B2C, retailers, distributers, manufacturers, fundraisers or professional service providers.

But the framework and key components remain constant. People are people after all. Sometimes in the rush for short-term profit, it's easy to forget that most organisations essentially consist of humans working to create value for other humans. Getting fit for digital means putting people first: you, your colleagues, your supply chain partners and the people who buy your products and services.

Digital technology simply bestows extra power to help us to become more superhuman in the way in which we find and serve our customers. It has already changed how, as producers, we can create value and, as consumers, how we perceive it and even participate in its creation. But the tech alone will never be a silver bullet to competitive supremacy. The future must be bionic, an integration of humans and technology, using the best of both to deliver the goods.

As the number of face-to-face interactions in business dwindle, we need to work harder to humanise our relationships with our customers. We need to think about sales, revenue, costs and ROI, of course. We have to make a profit. But we also need to think more about what Ted Rubin called the "return on relationship", both for our staff and our customers.

Counter-intuitively perhaps, technology can help us to humanise and deepen those relationships. It can also provide extra horsepower, but, like the famous tyre manufacturer said, power is nothing without control. Leaders won't get control by micro-managing in a digital business. There are too many moving parts for that now. It will just slow things up. They must coach more and play less. They must use technology to remain in control at a distance, having set the conditions for success by developing the organisation's core strengths.

Those core strengths are the vision, the culture and the strategy. They are the deep understanding of customers and their journey to purchase; a recognition that the customer experience reaches far beyond the product or service itself. Leaders must show a clarity of purpose and an inquisitive mindset, always seeking opportunities to innovate and get more of the right things done better and faster.

For many companies, the sales and marketing function is likely to be in the vanguard of their digital evolution. But digital affects every function across an organisation because everybody has an influence on the customer's experience of interacting with you. Business has always been a team game, but in a digital world the need for everybody to work together is magnified. Marketeers can't be left to obsess about the customer on their own.

Now everybody in the organisation must join them. That includes Angie in accounts and David in dispatch. If that refund isn't processed or that item doesn't arrive on time, your perceived value will be negatively impacted, just as much as when your shiny new website is too slow or too difficult to use, or your disconnected services suffer from customer amnesia. It's all part of the customer experience and those customers are now very demanding. They expect everything to be easy, and there is nothing that requires more thought and planning than easy.

Leaders must be fully committed and ensure that they acknowledge the real fears and inertia that are typical, when change is perceived as a threat to power bases and even livelihoods. They must expend as much energy into warming up a team for change as they expend on the search for, and technical implementation of, new tools. More than that, change must be framed in a language and context that everyone within an organisation can relate to and buy into.

Getting fit for digital is a process that recognises that mindset is more important than a rigid plan, as long as the business core is strong and well-defined. It acknowledges that closer collaboration and new skills are necessary to get the digital power down effectively where the rubber meets the road. It means that flatter, less hierarchic team formations are required to reduce drag. It is essential that those closest to the customer in an organisation are empowered to take decisions, based on easily accessible, relevant and accurate data.

That doesn't negate the need to make good technology decisions. It's technology that helps us ordinary mortals to become bionic business superhumans. So, business leaders must keep in mind that the key elements of a modern technology strategy are cloud-hosted, mobile-first, insights-driven and for many, loosely coupled. Those are the ingredients for the creation of a winning customer experience platform that delivers across every device and screen size. They are the building blocks for building an agile culture where continuous innovation, driven by data, becomes part of an organisation's DNA.

Over the years I have seen how digital has made organisations of all types and sizes become better places to buy from, work with and work within. I have also seen how outdated management structures, old school skills and analogue mindsets, inhibit the pursuit of greater productivity. I have learned that the struggle to fit the square peg of traditional business practices into the round hole of a new digital business context is doomed to fail.

Not every business is experiencing the heat yet. Some do not feel that they are standing on a burning platform. It is taking longer for new business or operating models to become pervasive in some market verticals, particularly those where a major disrupter has yet to come knocking, with a threat to blow the house down.

Like getting physically fit, unless you face an existential threat, there are always plenty of good reasons to put it off. But time is beginning to run out for those who have yet to get to grips with the impact that digital will have on their livelihoods in the coming years. It's time for all business leaders to put the periscope up, take a good look at the horizon and get their organisations fully fit for digital business.

Digital should be the catalyst for a business reboot. Done in the right way, with proper planning, it doesn't have to hurt. In fact, it can be an extremely positive process that leaves your people feeling energised, focused and motivated about your new digital business blueprint. Tackling issues head-on, unblocking log-jams and having a clear vision breathes fresh air into organisations. In a digital world that's advancing every day is there really a choice? Just get started and trust the process. You'll know when you've arrived because new agile ways of working become a business habit, a muscle memory, helping your team to react effectively to any opportunities and challenges that come your way. As Jack Welch said, "If the rate of change on the outside exceeds the rate of change on the inside, the end is near".

Need-to-know workout tips: ten benefits of getting fit for digital business

1   Look better: become more attractive to customers and employees.
2   Feel better: reduce stress and create a better quality of working life.
3   Stay mentally sharp: improve customer focus, prioritisation, innovation and competitiveness.
4   Be more productive: increase revenue, ROI and profit.
5   Develop faster reactions and increased agility: seize opportunities and overcome challenges.
6   Improve circulation: improve business flow with better processes.

7   Boost balance and co-ordination: more collaboration and less siloed activity.
8   Help to control weight: stay lean and efficient.
9   Strengthen the immune system: improve resilience, security and business health.
10 Combat the effects of ageing: stay relevant to your connected audiences.

In sum, live better for longer: survive and thrive as a digitally fit business growing revenue and profit while improving organisational health and well-being.

Bibliography

Rubin, Ted. (2011) Return on Relationship™: The New Measure of Success (5 April). Available at https://tedrubin.com/return-on-relationship-the-new-measure-of-success/ (accessed 11 February 2018).

Welch, J. and Welch, S. (2014). *Winning*. HarperCollins e-Books.

Epilogue

I am going to round off with a short case study of how a traditional office furniture manufacturer has begun its journey to digital business fitness.

I won't name it, but the company has a long and proud history stretching back more than a century. Some of its team members have given more than forty years of service. In recent times, however, it has come under significant pricing pressure from other suppliers across the world. These competitors are working with a much lower cost base and have become much more visible to potential customers worldwide via the World Wide Web. Inevitably, these changes in the competitor landscape and consumer behaviour have negatively impacted the company's B2B and B2C sales and margins.

The leadership team had their moment of truth. They understood that customers' purchasing behaviours, and the power balance between buyer and supplier, had shifted. There was a recognition of the need for deep change – to adapt or die. They chose to adapt. They knew that they couldn't do it on their own, so they forged new partnerships and developed new products. They integrated with another company specialising in office communication technology and began to design custom-made office furniture fit for modern organisations. They became more customer-centric, working with their clients to understand how they could meet their twenty-first-century office furniture needs.

The result was a new generation of *connected* office furniture. For example, the manufacturer produced meeting tables with seamlessly integrated touch screens and features that allowed meeting participants to wirelessly connect their smartphones or laptops. Its suite of products also made it easier for remote participants to be "in the room" through integrated video conferencing.

The business leadership also invested in team alignment, undertaking practical steps to warm up their people for change. They worked with a consultant to run a series of workshops, designed to develop a shared vision for the company's future and to foster inter-departmental collaboration and alignment.

The board also began to develop a new business model and, realising that it could not be supported by decades-old structures and processes, they began an ongoing programme to reinvent their inner workings. They invested in training to develop modern management and digital business skills, as well as reorganising their structures. They have been adopting and adapting Agile methodologies, with self-governed teams operating with less command and control. For example, they turned their account managers into product owners and internal client representatives.

That business has already come a long way on its journey to digital fitness. It isn't finished and it hasn't been without challenges en route. But the important thing is that it has begun. The company is learning more every day about what it means to be in shape to thrive in the digitally dominated future. It is now catching up with its customers and getting ahead of its competitors – and your organisation can do the same.

Index